J. O. N. Perkins is Professor of Economics at the University of Melbourne. He has also been a Research Fellow at the Australian National University, and has worked on the editorial staff of the *Economist*.

THE MACROECONOMIC MIX TO STOP STAGFLATION

THE MACROECONOMIC MIX TO STOP STAGFLATION

J. O. N. Perkins

Professor of Economics
University of Melbourne

A HALSTED PRESS BOOK

JOHN WILEY & SONS
New York

First published 1979 by
THE MACMILLAN PRESS LTD
London and Basingstoke

Published in the U.S.A. by
HALSTED PRESS,
a Division of John Wiley & Sons, Inc.,
New York

Photoset in Great Britain by
Bristol Typesetting Co Ltd, Bristol
Printed in Great Britain

Library of Congress Cataloging in Publication Data

Perkins, James Oliver Newton.
The macroeconomic mix to stop stagflation.

"A Halsted Press book."
1. Economic policy. 2. Inflation (Finance) and unemployment. I. Title
HD82.P4437 1979 339·5 78-13733
ISBN 0-470-26525-6

To the *PM, whoever he or she may be*

Contents

Preface

My main debt in the writing of this book has been to the many academic and official economists—nearly two hundred of them—in sixteen countries and several international organisations who were tolerant enough to allow me to try out my ideas on them in the course of visits to Western Europe, North America, Japan, India and Singapore in 1976–7—in addition to many in Australia. Without their comments—both critical and helpful—I would not have had the confidence to put my ideas into print.

Among my colleagues at the University of Melbourne I owe a special debt to Ian McDonald, who refused to let me get away with shifting the aggregate supply curve by means of monetary policy without adequate logical foundation, and who, together with David Vines, finally helped me to find a sustainable argument for doing so.

In addition to these two, who have commented on parts of various drafts, I have benefited also from comments made by Richard D. Freeman, Dennis Mahoney and Sam Soper; and also from comments by Kwang Ng, whose work on the theoretical aspects of changing the mix I discovered at a late stage in my work. His rigorous exposition (so far unpublished) of the implications of what I would call the cost-push aspects of high tax rates takes the matter much further than I would have been capable of doing. I am naturally solely responsible for remaining deficiencies.

Mrs Rosemary Thompson typed from an often difficult manuscript with admirable speed and efficiency.

Don Frearson gave me valuable assistance with proof-reading.

J.O.N.P.

London, March 1978

1 Introduction

During recent years the world economy has been plagued by the dual problem of inflation and unemployment. To a considerable extent the problem has been manmade; for governments in many major countries have been reluctant—rather than unable—to take the measures necessary to raise the level of activity to nearer the economic potential of their economies, because they believe that only by holding down the level of activity (that is, generally by holding up the level of unemployment and of spare capacity) can they restrain the rate of inflation.

The main contention of this book is, by contrast, that there is available a combination of measures that would enable governments to hold down the rate of inflation, and even to return to price stability if the process were taken far enough, without continuing to make the large sacrifices of output, and so of economic welfare, that have been made in the past few years—and yet without relying solely or mainly (and perhaps not even at all) on some form of voluntary or compulsory prices and incomes policy.

It will be argued that success in restraining inflation at any given level of activity will depend upon the particular combination of monetary and budgetary measures employed by a government. It will not be contended that policies directed at holding down the rate of inflation by holding up the level of unemployment will necessarily fail to check inflation: they may, or may not, succeed, depending partly on the 'mix' or blend of macroeconomic measures —monetary and budgetary policy, and measures such as exchange rate policy—with which they are applied. But this is also true of measures directed at raising the level of operation of the economy of a country up closer to 'full employment'. Taken by itself, and holding 'everything else equal' one might expect that a policy that raised the level of activity would tend to raise prices and the rate of inflation. But the kernel of the argument of this book is that the other things need not remain equal; that it is perfectly possible in principle so to change the combination of monetary and budgetary measures employed, whilst taking steps to raise the level of activity, that this change of mix can have as much downward pressure on the price level as any upward effect on prices that results from operating the economy at nearer to full employment.

It is not a contention of this book that prices and incomes policies are either necessary, inevitable, useless or harmful, though they may in fact be any of these things in particular countries at particular times, depending largely on the form they take. But it will be argued that any prices and incomes policies that are adopted will have a greater chance of success, and the best hope of doing more good than harm, if the mix of monetary and budgetary measures chosen to accompany them is such as to hold down the price level.

In contrast to the mix of measures to be proposed here, the setting of the main macroeconomic instruments chosen in most major countries in recent years has been such as to generate a high rate of inflation whilst also making it harder to reduce unemployment without causing a faster rise in the price level. Governments generally have kept tax rates too high and have been unwilling to provide people with adequate supplies of attractive financial assets in which to hold their savings. The process of changing the mix in the opposite direction that will be proposed in the ensuing chapters should be acceptable to people with a wide range of views on most matters of macroeconomic policy. The proposals are not distinctively 'monetarist' or 'anti-monetarist'. They share the 'monetarist' view that it is dangerous to ignore the growth of the money supply. But the view to be put forward strongly contests the aspect of 'monetarist' views that seems to have been most widely accepted by governments—namely, that the curtailment of the level of activity is a *necessary* price to pay in order to lower people's expectations of the future rate of inflation. Such a policy may or may not succeed: but, even if it can succeed, it is not *necessary* to pay this price in lost output and other social costs if, as this book contends, there is a way of doing the same thing that does not involve permitting a high level of unemployment.

The proposals are preceded by a very brief outline (Chapter 2) of the nature and operation of the various measures available to governments to deal with macroeconomic problems. Those with any systematic knowledge of macroeconomics will probably not find it necessary, or even useful, to read this chapter, but those who doubt their familiarity with the nature of the main macroeconomic weapons should use this chapter as a starting-point.

A simplified form of the proposals is outlined in Chapter 3, where they are applied to the context of a 'closed' economy, which may best be thought of as the world as a whole, though it serves also as a first base for discussing the problems of individual 'open' economies—that is, an individual country conducting international payments with the rest of the world. In this chapter the approach is to consider ways of reducing the price level, and so the rate of inflation, *without changing the level of activity*. This initial approach is adopted partly as a simplifying expository device; and partly because it may be easier to persuade governments to start with an approach of this sort, rather than to apply the principles initially to the more complex problem of raising the level of activity without generating a higher rate of inflation than they are prepared to tolerate.

But once the principles are accepted, they can be applied to the task of overcoming 'stagflation'—that is, to solving the problem of too high a level of unemployment combined with too rapid a rate of inflation; and this problem is considered in Chapter 4. In Chapter 5 consideration is given to some complications and possible limitations of the process of applying the suggested principles. Some of the objections that people may raise are also discussed; although they are found generally to be misconceived, several of them may nevertheless be very significant in the sense of being serious potential political obstacles to securing general acceptance of the sort of policies that are being proposed.

Chapter 6 outlines the qualifications and elaborations of the proposals that are necessary if they are to be applied by the government of an open economy (which means, by any individual country) having, as it does, not only additional economic instruments but also additional problems that are not present in a closed economy. In particular, the question of exchange rate policy is covered in this chapter.

Finally, in Chapter 7 some implications of the proposals for international arrangements, especially international monetary arrangements, are discussed. Essentially, the problem is that of devising international arrangements to assist and encourage countries to pursue macroeconomic policies that will be in the interests of all of them. The principal conclusions for macroeconomic policy-making are also outlined in this chapter.

2 Macroeconomic Policy: The 'Orthodox' Approach

Virtually all countries now share the problem of trying to prevent serious inflation without bringing about a considerable decline in the rate of economic growth and living standards. The problem is therefore one that needs to be considered in a global context. But as there is no world government it may appear unrealistic to ask what economic policies ought to be adopted for the world as a whole. There are, however, two principal justifications for adopting this approach initially. The first is that unless individual national governments bear in mind the need to approach this problem on a world basis, it is highly unlikely that any of them will successfully achieve the broad aims of macroeconomic policy which are important to them. The second principal justification for beginning with this approach is that it underlines many factors which are important in each individual country, namely those that abstract from the complications of its transactions with the rest of the world. In other words this 'closed economy' approach is relevant both for the world as a whole and also to some extent for each individual country (especially large ones). But for individual countries it is relevant only as a first step in the exposition, which may, indeed, need to be greatly modified when account is taken of a country's transactions with the rest of the world. These complications of an 'open economy' must always be borne in mind in making prescriptions for policy for individual countries.

For many years (since approximately the beginning of the Second World War in some countries) the analytical framework underlying prescriptions for macroeconomic policy in most industrialised Western countries has been based largely on Keynes's contributions to economic thought in the depression of the 1930s, and their development to handle problems of excess demand in the early 1940s. Up to the early 1970s, this approach seemed to be a more or less sufficient basis for thinking about macroeconomic policy, though it has in recent years been greatly elaborated. In itself it continues to be essential, but the approach in terms of influencing the overall level of demand now seems inadequate in a world of simultaneous unemployment and serious inflation, where it needs complementing by equal emphasis on the choice of the 'mix' of measures that are to be applied to establish the desired level of activity.

It remains important, however, that the essential principles of the orthodox, established, approach should be understood and applied, but that they should not be given the almost exclusive role that has hitherto been accorded to them in policy formulation and in basic economics courses. The dominance of this approach in the training of economists and policy-makers generally during the past two or three decades has probably made it especially difficult for them to adapt their thinking to new problems and to changes in the institutional framework in which they have to operate.

This chapter summarises the 'orthodox' or 'traditional' approach to the formulation of macroeconomic policy.

POLICY IN A CLOSED ECONOMY

The main aim of the policy-maker in a closed economy is to keep the level of total demand in the economy 'at about the right level'. If it is too low, an unacceptably high level of unemployment will result; if it is too high, total demand for the available supply of goods and services will expand faster than total production can expand, so that an unacceptable amount of inflation will result. This situation is variously described as 'overfull employment' or 'excess demand'. The various types of expenditure—which, taken together, may be either inadequate or excessive—include all forms of consumption expenditure by individuals, investment expenditure by businesses (on plant, equipment and so on), and government spending on goods and services. The only source of supply available to meet these demands in a closed economy is its own production. The instruments with which the government can attempt to influence demand in a closed economy are: its own spending, including transfer payments such as pensions and subsidies; tax rates; and monetary policy. It may also be able to influence total demand by applying certain types of direct controls; but unless these are very extensive they are more likely to affect the direction of spending and output than the total of all forms of spending. If unemployment is 'too high' governments should take steps to raise total demand; if inflation is 'too rapid' they should adopt measures to reduce expenditure.

For many years during the 1960s there was a widely accepted view that governments had considerable freedom as to what combination of rates of inflation and levels of unemployment they should choose. In other words, there was not just a particular level of demand (relative to capacity) at which inflation became too rapid, but a range of levels of employment (or unemployment) over which the rate of inflation changed, with relatively lower levels of inflation being associated with relatively higher rates of unemployment. The precise relationship between the two objects of macroeconomic policy might vary, from country to country and also from time to time, and especially according to the precise stage of the trade cycle at which the economy was at any given time (and according to whether activity was rising or falling relative to capacity). This became known as the 'Phillips' curve.[1]

Different countries might choose different combinations of inflation and unemployment, whether because their preferences varied between these two objectives, or because the 'tradeoff' between the two varied from one country to another—a greater increase in the rate of unemployment being necessary in order to reduce the rate of inflation by a given percentage in one country (or period) than was required in another. But governments were in the 1960s thought to have considerable freedom to choose from a 'menu' of possible choices between rates of unemployment and inflation. A few voices were raised to suggest that what now seem to be the rather low rates of inflation (by more recent standards—though not by those of earlier decades) experienced during the 1950s and 1960s could not continue for long without leading to more rapid rates of inflation; and that greater efforts should be made to achieve real price stability, perhaps by holding down total demand. But generally governments felt that it was a sufficient guide to policy to aim at a level of demand that was 'about right': and macroeconomists generally felt up to the late 1960s that the types of economic problems in which they specialised were more or less solved, except for certain difficulties of timing the adjustment of the various weapons in such a way as to minimise either serious inflation or serious unemployment.

The various types of measures used for restraining demand or for stimulating it (as was felt to be appropriate) are usually outlined in basic books and courses as if they were alternatives that were all about equally acceptable. Some attention has been given to criteria for deciding between them: but it is fair to say that these criteria are seldom or never brought together and emphasised in most basic books on the subject. If the world were one in which the rate of inflation depended solely on the level of demand (relative to capacity) the precise mix of measures whereby 'full employment' was maintained would obviously not matter from this point of view: and this approach has been typical of both the attitude of policy-makers and of the writers of most of the books on which education in economics has been based. The principal theme of this book is, by contrast, to emphasise the principles that need to be applied in choosing which of the available instruments to vary in order to affect the level of demand with the minimum upward effect (or the maximum downward effect) on the rate of inflation.

BUDGETARY AND MONETARY MEASURES

The first of the available measures for affecting demand in a closed economy is the level of government spending. By increasing government expenditure on goods and services, the level of demand, and therefore job opportunities, can normally be increased. The most expansionary effect is achieved if this is financed by the creation of money—rather than by borrowing from the public; but some expansion may still be obtainable if the extra spending is financed by the raising of extra loans by the government (though some economists would contest this view). Similarly, extra jobs may well be created even if the extra spending by the government is offset by extra tax receipts; for these may be paid partly out of what people would otherwise have saved, so that the fall in the number of jobs resulting from the reduction in the expenditure of the taxpayers may not be as great as the rise in jobs resulting from the extra government spending. In any event, total employment will rise when the government spends on goods and services as much as it takes away in taxes, provided that the recipients of the extra incomes so created consume the same proportion of the extra income as do the individuals who pay the extra taxes.

At the second and subsequent rounds of expenditure further jobs will normally be created, as the people employed by the extra government spending increase their own consumption, and then subsequently as others also increase their consumption as a result of being provided with jobs through the spending of these consumers, and so on (the so-called 'multiplier' effects). Investment spending by business may also rise as a result of this extra consumption expenditure as the capacity of industry becomes more fully stretched. Business expenditure on investment may also be stimulated by the payment of subsidies or by granting tax concessions.

Much the same effect can be achieved by extra government spending on transfer payments—such as pensions. But in this case there is no creation of jobs 'at the first round'—that is, until the recipients spend it. The effects therefore depend on how far the recipients themselves choose to spend the extra receipts.

In the same way, increases or decreases of tax rates—which are analogous to changes in transfer payments in the other direction—can also be used to affect total demand. For changes in tax rates, as for changes in transfer payments, the total effect on the level of demand and employment depends primarily on what proportion of the disposable income taken away from them (or given to them) affect the saving of taxpayers (or recipients); and on the similar decisions of those whose incomes are affected by these decisions of the original recipients or taxpayers.

In all these cases of changes in the budget, there may or may not be a simultaneous decision to borrow more or less from the public or to create more or less money. In fact, most budgetary decisions are accompanied by some decisions about the methods of financing the budgetary changes, which have some monetary effect. At one extreme, there are some economists who have stressed the role of the budget so far as to suggest, or to argue, or to imply, that the effects of changes in the money supply are almost insignificant by comparison. At the other extreme are some 'monetarist' economists who argue that only if the money supply is changed at the same time are budgetary decisions likely to have an appreciable effect on the level of demand. The revival of this latter view was perhaps a natural reaction against the more extreme view in the other direction, which had itself sprung from certain passages in Keynes's writings where he himself was concerned to correct what he felt to be an excessive emphasis given by his predecessors to the effects of changes in monetary policy. The more reasonable view seems to be to keep one's mind open to the possibility that in a particular country, or a particular set of circumstances, either monetary or budgetary measures may be the more reliable and predictable in their effects on demand and employment; that they are generally best varied together; but that some discretion is available to a government as to the precise combinations of these measures that it can choose in order to have a given effect on demand.

The Use of Monetary Policy

Without necessarily changing the setting of its budgetary instruments a government can affect total demand by changing the setting of monetary policy. It may do this by purchasing or selling bonds (or other assets) in the open market, or by placing the banking system in a position to lend more, or less, freely. It thus makes it easier or harder for borrowers to finance spending, and so influences the level of demand, particularly that for capital goods including housing and durable consumer goods. It may also be able to influence the lending undertaken by certain types of non-bank financial intermediaries, and the use made of hire-purchase or other consumer-financing facilities, and so to have an appreciable (if temporary) effect on total demand through this channel. If its efforts to influence bank lending are concentrated on quantitative controls over bank liquidity or bank lending this may have the effect of encouraging lending and borrowing through other channels, and its attempts also to control these channels directly may simply cause borrowers to avoid these controls by borrowing elsewhere—like a balloon bulging out at a different point when it is pushed in at one or two places. For this reason, the more general and the more market-oriented are the monetary (and similar) measures applied, the more likely is it that they will be effective in influencing total demand. It is true that measures to reduce the money supply may be in part—or sometimes perhaps even wholly—offset by people turning over the existing money supply more rapidly; but there are limits to which the effects on demand of a contraction in the money supply can and will be offset in this way, especially in the relatively short run.

Furthermore, any such process of 'speeding up the velocity of circulation' has to operate by means that involve some borrowers in offering more attractive terms to people with idle balances, in order to persuade them to reduce their cash balances; and if the potential borrowers can do this it is also open to governments to compete for such funds by offering sufficiently attractive terms to lenders. If monetary policy turns out to be ineffective, therefore, it is usually because governments are unable or (more probably) unwilling to offer sufficiently attractive terms to lenders to dissuade them from making more funds available to potential spenders. A sufficiently tough monetary policy can, then, usually be relied on to restrain demand. But, on the other hand, there remains room for doubt about how far the mere expansion of the available supplies of credit is likely to stimulate activity at the bottom of a serious recession, when lack of markets rather than lack of finance is the major restraint on business spending, and when lack of confidence is also probably the main constraint on consumer spending. Although major recessions of this sort were virtually absent between the 1930s and the mid-1970s, it has been widely accepted that this may be a limitation on the usefulness of monetary policy; and the need to use budgetary measures in such circumstances (at least in company with monetary measures) can reasonably be accepted as likely to remain relevant, at least in serious recessions, though probably not in minor ones.

The experience of the quarter-century following the Second World War suggested that governments needed to use all the instruments available to them, working in harmony, in order to affect the level of demand in the desired direction. At the very least, one could reasonably argue that if one tried to hold down interest rates artificially at a time when demand was too high, the pressure imposed on the available budgetary measures to restrain demand was likely to be intolerable—or at any rate that the severity of the budgetary measures required in such circumstances would be beyond what politicians would normally consider tolerable. But, on the other hand, one could reasonably expect that reliance on monetary measures alone to fulfil the role of stabilising demand was likely to be inadequate. Both groups of measures could, and normally should, be used in the same direction if governments were to affect the level of activity in the desired manner.

'Discretion Versus Rules of Thumb'

Doubts have been expressed—often by those economists who have also stressed the dominant role of monetary policy—about whether governments can and will vary the setting of macroeconomic instruments swiftly enough to maintain an adequate but not excessive level of demand. The tendency for governments to act too late, and then sometimes to do too much, led those of this view to advocate the application of such rules of thumb as 'a steady expansion of the money supply', as likely to hold the economy nearer to the path of stable growth than varying the setting of budgetary and monetary instruments according to what seems to be required at any given time. Most economists continue to favour the discretionary use of budgetary and monetary instruments, stressing—perhaps understandably and defensibly—that even if the timing of the use of such instruments has often been ill-judged in the past, there is no reason why governments should not learn from experience, and so achieve better results than by the application of any conceivable rule of thumb. In any event, the choice of the particular variables to be expanded at a steady rate—such as the money supply (on one of several possible definitions) or of liquid financial assets generally, and perhaps also of the level of government expenditure and tax receipts—presents a wide area of discretion in itself; and decisions to change the rate of growth of the variables selected would have to be made from time to time, with changing circumstances and experience, so that discretion would thus, in this respect also, be let in by the back door. In any event, there could always be doubts about how far the monetary or other financial targets selected could in fact be controlled at all precisely by the government or the central bank. In some circumstances a central bank may put the banks in a position to lend at a certain rate, but they may not be able to find enough borrowers whom they regard as creditworthy to be able to expand their lending fast enough; or else their potential customers might not be prepared to borrow at that rate.

Nevertheless, this issue of 'discretion versus rules of thumb' must still be regarded as a somewhat open one so long as governments have in many cases a bad record of varying their macroeconomic instruments in a timely way. It is easy to criticise any particular rule of thumb that can be suggested; but one can reasonably take the view that the record of success to be beaten is not an impressive one—especially in view of the very serious recession that the world has allowed itself to fall into during the 1970s. Prior to that, on the other hand, one could argue that there had been a long period of relatively well-sustained growth in the world economy, and that government policies might reasonably be given some credit for this. Yet, with the instruments available to them and the understanding that was supposed to have been reached in principle about the best way to use them, one could nevertheless argue that in many countries the record was not very impressive.

Perhaps a reasonable conclusion to be drawn from the 'discretion versus rules of thumb' controversy would be that if the expansion of the money supply (on any reasonable definition), or of broadly comparable financial aggregates, strays far outside certain limits (which should be related to the growth of the productive potential of the economy and to the rate of inflation considered both tolerable and feasible) it probably means that policy is in need of correction, and that a watch should always be kept on the growth of such aggregates—including that of government spending and tax receipts. The West German central bank, for example, announced a target range of growth rates for the monetary base in the mid-1970s. But rules of thumb of this sort can never relieve a government or a central bank from the use of a considerable degree of discretion; and when corrections are required it is usually wiser to introduce them earlier rather than later. The reason why discretion seems often to have failed is not necessarily that it has been used excessively, but more often than not because it has been exercised in the wrong way and at the wrong time (often for political reasons). A wide understanding of the role of macroeconomic instruments and the improvement in the quality of information about the state of the economy (and the speed with which the relevant information becomes available) should make it more likely in future that discretion in changing macroeconomic instruments will be exercised before it is too late. If some use is made in future of a range of target rates of growth for the principal financial aggregates, at least as warning signals that policy may be going astray (whether or not these are publicly announced), the extensive debate on 'rules-of-thumb versus discretion' could lead to a productive outcome in the form of a more timely application of macroeconomic instruments in many countries. There is, moreover, no reason why this conclusion should not stand when one comes to consider the application of more complex combinations of weapons and of other aims of macroeconomic policy in the open economy.

THE OPEN ECONOMY: BUDGETARY AND MONETARY MEASURES

In an open economy the government has to bear in mind the state of the country's balance of payments, and the level of its reserves.

Fluctuations in a country's external payments might be met entirely by allowing the price for its currency—the rate of exchange—to fluctuate like the price of any other commodity. But, in practice, governments usually intervene in the foreign exchange market (to a greater or lesser extent) to influence the rate of exchange. They do this by holding a stock of foreign currencies, which they make available to the country's residents when receipts of foreign exchange are falling short of what the country wishes to pay to the residents of other countries: and they add to the reserves in those periods when receipts of foreign exchange are unusually high in relation to the demand for them.

If the reserves fall unduly low, confidence in the country's currency will fall sharply, and eventually the country may have insufficient by way of international liquidity to meet its needs to pay for imports and to make other payments to the rest of the world. But if the reserves are allowed to rise to an unnecessarily high level the country is thereby foregoing the use of real resources (by way of potential imports) that it might have used to meet some of the needs of its residents. In an open economy, therefore, unless a government is willing to allow the exchange rate to fluctuate with complete freedom it has to concern itself with the additional macroeconomic objective of ensuring an adequate but not excessive level of reserves, and seeing that the state of the country's balance of payments will be consistent with the maintenance of an appropriate level of the reserves in the present and prospective future.

All the measures of monetary and budgetary policy that we have so far discussed may be employed partly with the aim of influencing the state of the balance of payments. Any of these measures that are used with the aim of stimulating demand—such as a reduction in tax rates, a rise in government spending, or an easing of monetary policy—will also tend to raise the level of imports (at any given rate of exchange), as activity rises. The level of exports may also be reduced as a result of the diversion of effort from the production of exports to the production of goods for the home market when activity expands. Expansionary measures are thus likely to worsen the current account of the balance of payments, and to that extent to reduce the level of the reserves. There may also be effects through capital account transactions. The expansion of activity that results from these measures makes overseas investors more inclined to lend to the country undertaking the expansion, and residents of that country more eager to borrow overseas. On the other hand, the weakening of the country's balance of payments on current account may make the residents of other countries less willing to invest in the country undertaking the expansion, if they fear that this may eventually reduce the level of its reserves and so perhaps lead in future to a depreciation of its currency in foreign exchange markets. So far as the inflow of capital is affected by the level of interest rates in the country, the adoption of expansionary budgetary measures (which tend to raise interest rates) is more likely to lead to a greater net inflow of capital (or a smaller net outflow), as it makes the country a more profitable place than before in which to lend, and a more expensive place in which to borrow. On the other hand, expansionary monetary measures (which are more likely to operate in a direction that holds down interest rates) will to that extent operate in the direction of discouraging capital inflow.

If a country's reserves are high and its balance of payments strong, it may welcome the balance of payments effects of the adoption of expansionary measures. But if it is troubled simultaneously by high unemployment and by low reserves (or a weak balance of payments), any expansionary monetary and budgetary measures that it adopts with the aim of reducing the level of unemployment will make the external situation worse. It would then be in a 'dilemma' situation, where anything it does by way of monetary or budgetary measures to solve its internal macroeconomic problem will make its external problem worse. This would also be true if it was in a position of excessive balance of payments surplus combined with excess demand; for budgetary or monetary measures taken with the aim of reducing the level of domestic spending would then tend also to make its balance of payments surplus still greater.

THE OPEN ECONOMY: EXPENDITURE-SWITCHING INSTRUMENTS

But in an open economy a government has also certain additional instruments with which it can affect the state of the balance of payments at any given level of activity; so that by using these it can to a considerable extent avoid unwanted effects on its balance of payments if it takes expansionary (or contractionary) measures of monetary or budgetary policy. One should not look upon these so-called 'expenditure-switching' measures, such as alterations of its exchange rate, the general level of tariffs, or general import controls, as being especially directed towards the state of the country's balance of payments, although the fact that they bear the appearance of having an especially direct impact on international transactions usually makes people think of them as in some way especially relevant to the external objectives of macroeconomic policy. In fact, however, all instruments of macroeconomic policy have an impact on all the macroeconomic objectives.

Just as monetary and budgetary measures affect not only the level of domestic activity but also the state of the balance of payments, in the same way a devaluation ('or depreciation') of the currency (that is, a reduction in the amount of foreign exchange that a unit of it will purchase) will not only tend to improve the balance of payments by discouraging purchases of imports, and usually also by making exports more competitive in terms of external currencies, but in the process of doing this the devaluation will increase the demand for home-produced goods and services, and so tend to raise the level of domestic activity. The same would be true if there were a rise in the general level of tariffs (or if other measures were taken to reduce imports directly); for not only would the reserves then tend to be higher as a result of the fall in imports, but the level of domestic activity will tend to rise, as a result of the switching of demand from imports towards home-produced substitutes. A devaluation will therefore normally be appropriate in a situation where activity and employment are low and the balance of payments is weak; whereas this is, as we saw above, a 'dilemma' situation from the viewpoint of monetary and budgetary policy, as the expansionary monetary and budgetary measures that are desirable in order to reduce unemployment would tend to make the balance of payments situation worse.

In the same way, an appreciation or a cut in tariffs is normally appropriate when the reserves are strong and the level of employment high—a situation where a contractionary monetary or budgetary policy would make the external problem of surplus worse in the process of eliminating the excess demand within the country.

There is, therefore, in principle, some combination of budgetary and monetary measures with expenditure-switching measures that ought to be able to reconcile the achievement of a high (but not excessive) level of activity with an adequate (but not excessive) level of a country's international reserves. One of the difficulties, however, is to decide what setting of the available instruments will achieve these aims. Another is that there may be doubts about how far and how soon a devaluation, or measures to reduce imports or to encourage exports, will have their effects.

But a further problem (as we shall see later) arises because the basic macroeconomic problem within countries is no longer merely a matter of the level of employment, but also of the rate of inflation: so that measures that are intended to raise activity may not only worsen the balance of payments but also raise the rate of inflation; and, at the same time, a measure, such as a devaluation, that is intended to improve the balance of payments and perhaps at the same time to stimulate activity, may also have the unwanted effect of raising the rate of inflation.

For these and other reasons, the use of the traditional macroeconomic measures in the manner outlined in this chapter has become an insufficient guide to solving the basic macroeconomic problems. It remains true, however, that it is important to understand the rationale underlying the way in which these measures have been used in the past (and are still generally used today) with the purpose of achieving the aims of macroeconomic policy.

But the coexistence of inflation and unemployment has in many countries led to the adoption of some form of 'prices and incomes' policies, with the aim of reducing the rate of inflation (at any given level of unemployment or activity). Such measures are largely based on the view that inflation has resulted partly from cost-push factors, such as 'trade union militancy'—to some extent independent of the level of unemployment. It is doubtful whether such views could be accorded the status of 'accepted orthodoxy', in the same way as can the principles of macroeconomic policy outlined in the present chapter; but they have certainly influenced policy greatly in many countries. It will be argued in the next chapter that the choice of an inappropriate mix of measures can lead to upward pressure on money wage rates and other money incomes. It is an open question whether there are also other (perhaps 'sociological' or 'non-economic') factors that are partly responsible for 'wage-push' (or 'income-push') inflation; or how far the adoption of more appropriate combinations of monetary and budgetary measures would be likely to solve the problem.

CONCLUSION

As high rates of inflation came to be associated with high rates of unemployment in the mid-1970s, the basic approach adopted in the past to restraining inflation became clearly insufficient. For attempts to restrain inflation by deflating the economy naturally tended to cause still higher levels of unemployment, and this was the major reason for the occurrence of the worst postwar recession in the world economy during 1974–8. One could argue that the process of checking inflation by holding down demand was merely taking longer to have the expected effect, presumably because the expectation of inflation had become deeply ingrained in most people's minds after many years of inflation, and after several years of very high inflation (by postwar standards) from the late 1960s onwards. Adherence to deflationary policies—in the USA and Japan, for example—during 1974–5 seemed to confirm that some success could be achieved in checking inflation by letting the level of unemployment remain high for a while; but there was naturally widespread reluctance to resort to this method of checking inflation; and there were in many countries continued doubts about its effectiveness, or at least about the social costs of relying solely on this method. At the very least, in a situation where inflation coexists with unemployment, it is natural to ask whether this orthodox approach should be supplemented by additional principles of macroeconomic policy-making, directed at giving the policy-maker advice about how to combine the successful checking of inflation with the minimum of unemployment and of other social costs. Whatever the contribution that can be made by prices and incomes policies, there is inevitably a dilemma whenever there is both a high level of unemployment and a high rate of inflation: for in that situation any policy measure on the demand side that will do something to help on one front is virtually certain to make things worse on the other, at least for a while. But some policy measures may be more likely than others to plunge an economy deep into this dilemma, whilst others may give greater hope of extraction from it. No government is likely to be able to dispense with operation on the general level of demand as part of its policy. This may still in future have to be given the greatest weight, but it may well henceforth be just one of the two essential principles of macroeconomic policy, with decisions about the precise 'mix', or combination, of macroeconomic measures to be adopted having a more or less equally important bearing on the amount of unemployment prevailing and also on the rate of inflation. The next chapter is therefore devoted to considering the principles to be applied in choosing the most appropriate policy mix to achieve a given level of demand, at as low a price level or as low a rate of inflation as possible.

3 The Policy Mix in a Closed Economy

We have discussed in the preceding chapter the approach to formulating macroeconomic policy in a closed economy which has in the period during and since the Second World War constituted the basis for most macroeconomic policy decisions in most major developed countries of the non-Communist world. The principal emphasis has usually been placed on securing the appropriate overall effect on demand by means of the government's budgetary and monetary measures.

The main contention of the present chapter is that attention to the effects of measures on the overall level of demand is not a sufficient basis for proper policy decisions in a world where inflation is continuing at an uncomfortably rapid rate even in economies with an undesirably high level of unemployment. Even if one accepts the view that a sufficient degree of restraint on the overall level of demand can eventually reduce inflation to tolerable levels with only low social costs, in the shape of lost output and social suffering, it must in any case be desirable to consider ways and means of minimising whatever these costs will be. No-one can doubt that there must be some real cost to the community if a government tries to restrain inflation by holding down the level of demand to below what would otherwise be regarded as full employment. It is true that if one believes such policies to be the only feasible, or the most promising, way of checking inflation one may fear that anything that suggests to politicians that there may be an easier way out would be better left unsaid. But it is better to face that risk, and to acknowledge that the choice of the particular combination—or 'mix'—of weapons used to achieve a given real effect on demand may itself affect the rate of inflation at any given level of activity; and the more the rate of inflation can be restrained by choosing a more appropriate mix of measures, the less will be the sacrifice of output and the loss of jobs required to bring down inflation to any given rate (even if this latter method would eventually be successful).

The present chapter is therefore concerned with discussing the relative effects on the rate of inflation at any given level of activity of choosing one particular combination of budgetary and monetary measures rather than some other. That is to say, it assumes that the government is aiming to maintain a particular level of real activity (which may be the existing one, or 'full employment', on some appropriate definition), and wishes to do this with as low a rate of inflation as possible. In fact, however, the lower the rate of inflation at any given level of activity, the nearer to full capacity is a government likely to feel able to permit the economy to operate. Success in minimising the rate of inflation at any given level of activity will therefore normally make it possible to operate the economy at nearer to 'full employment', and at consequently higher average levels of real income. This extension of the analysis will be made in the following chapter.

In this chapter and the two following ones the analysis is in terms of a 'closed' economy—that is, of one that has no transactions with the outside world. The adoption of this approach may be justified initially partly on the grounds that it is a simplification of reality which is a reasonable first approximation, even for a single 'open' economy in which foreign transactions are important. But the principal justification is that 'stagflation' has become a global problem, and that the adoption of an appropriate mix on a global scale is likely to be the main precondition for solving the problem. At the very least, the major countries would need to take the lead in adopting an appropriate mix; but, as we shall see in Chapter 6, even a small open economy can go far towards solving the problem by applying similar principles.

VARYING THE MIX

The macroeconomic instruments available to a government (in a closed economy) are the level of government spending, the level of tax rates, and the rate of growth of the money supply—which is influenced not only by the state of the budget, but also by the level of government borrowing from the public (or debt repayment) and by the rate of expansion of bank credit. By altering the setting of any one of these, the government could expect to change the total level of demand. We shall in this chapter be considering varying the setting of *two* of them at a time, with offsetting effects on the level of activity, in such a way as to leave the level of activity unchanged, and we shall be asking what effect this might be expected to have on the price level, or on the rate of inflation—which may be affected by the measures directly, and also indirectly if the change in the price level alters expectations about inflation; or in the sense that one or more successive changes in prices in one direction constitute a change in the rate of inflation during the period in which the prices change.

The mental bar to thinking about the simultaneous variation of two measures is that for so long we have thought mainly about making changes in these instruments one at a time, as ways of affecting total spending. (Moreover, in the past, when high rates of inflation usually coincided with excess demand, it normally did no obvious harm to vary both monetary and budgetary measures in the same direction; and a movement of either or both in the required direction was thus generally helpful.) It is, however, harder to juggle two balls than one (especially if one is trying to throw them in different directions); but it is essential to make the necessary mental effort to do so if we are to ask how the price level or the rate of inflation may be affected by a change in the mix of macroeconomic measures, *at a given level of activity.* (In the next chapter the analysis will be applied to the problem of bringing about a rise in activity with little or no upward effect on the price level or the rate of inflation.) In actual situations, a government has naturally to consider alternative settings of *all* the instruments available to it, and not merely of two or three: and it should be trying to find the combination of measures that will do most to hold down the price level or the rate of inflation at whatever level of activity is to be established. But the principles involved can be appreciated by considering alternative combinations of two of the main instruments at any one time.

We shall first consider what difference it is likely to make to the price level or the rate of inflation if, at a given level of activity, a government chooses a high level of both government spending and taxation, rather than pitching both the expenditure and revenue sides of the budget at a lower level.

We shall then compare two alternative settings of taxation and government borrowing from the public, assuming government spending to be kept at the same level in both alternatives.

Finally, we shall consider the effects of changing both the level of government spending and of government borrowing (with a given level of taxation).

THE PRICE LEVEL AND THE RATE OF INFLATION

Various policies suggested in the ensuing discussion for reducing the rate of inflation during a particular period may or may not also reduce the future rate of inflation after the point in time at which the change in policy is made. (In some theoretical discussions the term 'the rate of inflation' seems almost to have become identified with the latter concept, but its use will not be so limited in the ensuing discussion.) But, whilst a reduction in the future rate of inflation is usually one aim of policy, even a change of policy that causes only a once-and-for-all downward adjustment in the price level represents a fall in the rate of inflation over the period in which it occurs.

For the rate of inflation during a period reflects the successive price levels during that period. A given policy change that has a once-and-for-all effect in keeping the price level below what it would otherwise have been is thus perceived during the period in question as a change in the rate of inflation—though the theorist is rightly concerned to distinguish between policies that will have a lasting effect on the rate of inflation and those that will reduce it only temporarily by having a once-and-for-all effect on the price level. But those concerned with actual situations and policies cannot in practice distinguish at all exactly between these two effects. For what ought in principle to constitute a once-and-for-all downward effect on the price level may well affect people's expectations about the price level in future, and so the rate of inflation over some considerable period with which the policy-maker is concerned. We should certainly not assume that a given mix of measures will have a continued downward effect on the rate of inflation, if all that we can be sure of is that it will for some period reduce the price level. But for most policy-makers—and others—even a once-and-for-all downward pressure on prices will be worth having; and a measure that can be expected to have such an effect can in principle be repeated so long as further downward pressure on prices is desired; and downward effects on the price level constitute a clear change in the rate of inflation over the period in question.

In any event, the principles outlined in this book are concerned mainly with changing the mix, or 'blend' of macroeconomic measures in directions that may be expected to have a helpful effect in minimising either the rate of inflation, or the price level, or both, over some period or other; and to reduce the risk that the blend of measures adopted is one that works in the 'wrong' direction. Even once-and-for-all effects on the price level in the right direction (rather than in the wrong one) are therefore a reasonable aim of policy. The distinction between once-and-for-all effects on the price level and continuing effects on the rate of inflation becomes important, however, when it has to be decided whether repetitions of the dose of policy measures will be required; and whether or not that will carry increasing costs in some form or other. But very often it will be impossible to say how far a 'once-and-for-all' change in the price level will have some lasting effects on the rate of inflation: and some measures—notably a cut in cost-push taxes—may well have both effects. This should be borne in mind in interpreting all the subsequent discussion of effects of policy measures on either 'the price level' or 'the rate of inflation'.

THE MIX OF TAXATION AND GOVERNMENT SPENDING

Let us suppose that a government has decided what level of activity it wishes to see established over the period for which it is framing its budget. There are various combinations of taxes and government spending with which it could achieve any given level of real demand. (It could also use monetary policy and bond operations; but, for simplicity, attention is at present being focused on the possible settings of the budgetary instruments.)

If the government chooses to achieve the desired level of activity with a relatively high level of government spending it will have to impose a correspondingly higher level of tax rates (assuming that the setting of its other instruments is taken as given) than would be appropriate if it chose a lower level of government spending. For the greater are the demands made by the government sector on the resources of the economy the less there will be available for other purposes. If government spending is pitched at a high level, therefore, higher tax rates will be necessary (all else being equal) in order to keep total spending down to the target level for total (real) demand; whereas if government spending were lower, tax rates could, and should, also be correspondingly lower.

The crucial question is whether a 'high-level' budget (one with both high levels of government spending and high levels of taxation) will have more of a cost-push effect than one that embodies a lower level of both government spending and taxation. In recent years most governments and economists have come to accept that some taxes (at least) have some degree of 'cost-push' effect.[1] This may operate either through encouraging wage demands—through the effect of high indirect taxes on the cost of living, or through the stimulus to wage demands that may be given by high marginal tax rates on wage-earners. It may also operate through the effects of taxes on materials, components, equipment, fuels and employment (such as payroll taxes or social security contributions paid by the employer) on the prices charged by businesses. Where businesses are in a position to set their prices by some form of 'mark-up' or 'cost-plus' pricing, this is especially likely to occur. A high level of taxation on company profits may also have a cost-push effect. We need to know much more than we do about the relative cost-pushfulness of different taxes: but it is reasonable to argue that all taxes probably have some effect in this direction, though some types of tax presumably have good deal more than others.

A high level of taxation in relation to total output may well have not merely a once-and-for-all effect on the price level (when taxes rise to that level), but a persistent upward effect on wage rates and prices at a given level of activity. This is likely to occur when the effect of the high taxes is to make both wage (and salary) earners and producers more dissatisfied with their post-tax real incomes than they would otherwise be. This may lead unions to demand higher money wage-rates; if these are then paid, profit-earners may try to restore the real level of their post-tax incomes by raising the prices of their products. This naturally reduces the real post-tax incomes of wage-earners again, and they may then further raise their wage and salary demands; so that the process may persist so long as the tax-take leaves consumers highly dissatisfied with their post-tax real incomes.[2]

Of course, if the government reacts by holding down the rate of expansion of the money supply sufficiently, this process may be checked by a rise in unemployment, though it might require a very high level of unemployment and of spare capacity to prevent it. But whether the consequence is rapid inflation or high unemployment, or a mixture of the two, the problem for a government is the same: namely, to find a mix of measures that will be most likely to restrain the rise in prices and in money incomes without creating an otherwise undesirable and unnecessary rise in unemployment.

The problem of satisfying the real income demands of producers and employees may also be intensified by the reduction in productivity that may result from high tax rates. High tax rates (or at least some types of high taxes) may reduce the incentive to work and to take initiative and assume responsibility; they absorb manpower in the calculation of tax, in tax payment, and in tax collection, and lead to the employment of specialists in such generally socially useless occupations as tax avoidance (or tax evasion) and the use of time and energy for these purposes; and they may in other ways affect adversely the allocation of resources; in all these cases, the supply of goods and services available to satisfy the demands of producers and employees for inherently desirable marketable goods and services is correspondingly reduced at any given level of employment or activity, and therefore the likelihood of their making mutually inconsistent income claims, leading to continued inflation (unless they are checked by heavy unemployment) is correspondingly greater. Again, the high effective marginal tax rate often imposed when an unemployed person takes a job may reduce the willingness to find and accept employment. This tends to hold down real output and raise what some would call the 'natural' rate of unemployment. High tax rates may well then contribute to causing rapid rates of inflation or to stagflation; and a reduction in tax-rates may thus not merely bring about a once-and-for-all reduction in the price level but it may also cause a fall in the rate of inflation at any given level of activity.

It may reasonably be hoped that a reduction in tax rates will reduce these undesirable effects on living standards. If tax reductions increase people's willingness to work, to make innovations, to take initiative and assume responsibility; or if they result in the release of manpower from such basically useless occupations (from a social point of view) as tax-gathering and looking for loopholes in tax laws: the diversion of such energies as these to more fundamentally useful purposes will thus increase the efficiency with which the community uses its available resources, including its capital stock. It will also make available extra resources, some of which may be applied to increasing its future stock of capital, and to that extent help to raise living standards in future (even if the economy is operated at no nearer to its potential capacity than if the change of mix had not occurred). If the available supplies of useful real consumption goods and services is thereby increased it will, moreover, help to hold down the rate of inflation even if there is no change in the money income demands of producers and employees; and we have seen reason to believe that money income demands may in fact also be especially high and inconsistent when tax rates are high.

This means that a combination of measures which enables the level of taxation to be appreciably reduced (at any given level of activity) should have some effect in the direction of holding down the rate of inflation. In principle, one way in which this might be done is by a simultaneous reduction in both taxes and government spending. But this will not necessarily be the best way. For it is perfectly possible that all the government spending at present being undertaken is doing as much to maintain the level of productivity in the economy, and to hold down the rate of inflation, as would the use of the resources elsewhere in the economy. Only if the taxes reduced were ones that were keeping up the price level to a greater extent than it was being held down by the forms of government spending which would have to be curtailed would a change of mix towards a lower-level budget be helpful in reducing inflation. It may be reasonable to argue that the typical form of government spending does less to hold down the rate of inflation than the typical tax does to increase it. But this does not constitute a valid argument for slashing government spending generally with a view to making possible a reduction in tax rates. On both sides of the budget the reductions need to be carefully chosen. In any case, there are (as we shall see below) other ways of making possible reductions in tax rates, and these may be preferable to cuts in government spending.

SUBSIDIES AND TAXES

There is one form of government spending that may well be as effective in holding down the rate of inflation (at a given level of activity) as would be a cut of a similar order in some types of tax receipts. This is the instrument of government subsidies, especially those on items that figure prominently in the consumer's basic household spending, or those paid on certain constituents of business costs. For example, a government subsidy that enables a public authority to avoid putting up charges for public transportation may keep down the cost of living (as it is normally measured or commonly understood) at least as much as would a reduction in the indirect taxes imposed on some items of general consumption, such as beer, tobacco and certain foodstuffs. So far as wage demands are affected by the prices of such items, therefore, a high level of government subsidies on them may be as useful in holding down cost-push inflation as might some forms of tax cuts. Similarly, a subsidy on fuel used in businesses, or certain types of subsidy paid to businesses on the basis of the number of workers they employ, might do as much to hold down the prices charged by businesses for their products as would a reduction in the taxes paid by them. The greater the extent to which the businesses whose costs are affected by the subsidies (or taxes) are 'price-makers', rather than 'price-takers', the greater the likelihood that subsidies (like taxes) will affect the prices they charge.

THE MIX OF BOND SALES AND TAXATION

We have so far assumed that the government can vary only its expenditure and its tax receipts. But an alternative way of 'financing' a given level of government spending is by selling government securities to the public. The term 'financing' is to some extent a misnomer, as the value of bond sales or taxation required is not necessarily equal to the value of the government spending under consideration (though a rise in government spending must be financed by some combination of taxation, borrowing and money creation). One may therefore better describe this process as one of using bond operations to hold down the level of private expenditure sufficiently to make real resources available for the desired level of government spending. So far as the government chooses to sell more bonds to the public by offering them on more attractive terms, it will not be necessary to have such high tax rates. The sale of the more attractively priced bonds will thus make it possible to avoid some of the cost-push effect (or other undesirable effects) that would have been associated with the higher level of tax rates that would be the alternative to the extra sales of government bonds.

MONETARY POLICY AND THE PRICE LEVEL

There is another reason why a shift from tax-financing towards bond-financing may be expected to have some downward effect on the price level. The more expansionary is budgetary policy the lower the level of the money supply that will be required in order to maintain a given level of activity. A purely budgetary measure of expansion (such as a tax cut financed by an equal rise in bond sales), taken by itself would raise the level of activity; if activity were to be held constant, therefore, a correspondingly tighter monetary policy would be required, in order to curtail private spending sufficiently to keep activity from rising. A mix with a relatively expansionary budget will therefore involve a lower level of the money supply and higher real interest rates at any level of activity—whereas if that same level of activity had been established with a less expansionary budget (that is, with higher taxes or a lower level of government spending) the rate of increase in the money supply would have had to be greater, and real interest rates correspondingly lower.

We therefore need to ask whether the adoption of a mix with a relatively low money supply (and with consequently higher rates of interest) is likely to have a downward effect on the price level at any given level of activity. For if that is so, this constitutes an argument for a mix involving a tight monetary policy and an expansionary budgetary policy.

As the 'easy money' mix involves a higher level of the money supply, the natural expectation would be that it would involve a higher price level. Indeed, the association in most people's minds between high prices and a high money supply (or between a rapid rate of inflation and a rapid rise in the money supply) may be sufficient of itself to bring about this expected result. Even if this is all there is to the matter, it would be sufficient to justify the conclusions suggested here.

But it is not very satisfactory to rely on this argument that 'thinking makes it so'. For it is unlikely that such an expectation would persist if it had no rational basis. We need to ask, therefore, whether there are more fundamental reasons why a mix of measures involving a relatively high level of the money supply (and correspondingly lower interest rates) may be expected to mean a higher price level at a given level of activity.

There are various ways in which the particular mix of monetary and budgetary measures chosen to establish a particular level of activity might affect the price level.

One way in which this might occur would be if the adoption of a mix with fairly low interest rates (and a correspondingly larger money supply) leads people to bid up the prices of those types of real assets that become correspondingly more attractive as a result of the yield on financial assets being relatively low—and if this raises the general price level. Among those goods that people might be most likely to try to hold instead of financial assets would be real estate and commodities. Unless the output of these goods could be at once expanded in response to this shift in preferences (as interest rates fell) towards goods and away from financial assets the prices of these goods would tend to rise; and so far as their prices influenced costs of production generally, the price level of finished products would increase. The output of those types of goods that are fairly close substitutes for bonds would have to be relatively unresponsive to a rise in the demand for them, and such goods would have to be relatively important constituents of costs of production, for the general price level to be greatly raised as a result. But some rise in the price level is to be expected in any event.

There are also more general reasons why a mix involving a relatively large money supply (and correspondingly lower interest rates) at a given level of activity might be expected to be accompanied by a correspondingly higher price level. In a world where many producers, consumers, employers and employees have some degree of power to influence the level of prices and wage rates that they pay or accept, the level of their money holdings is likely to have some influence on pricing policy and wage settlements. (If, however, we were in a perfectly competitive world—on which most theoretical macroeconomic models seem to be based—this would generally not be true.) Perhaps this can best be seen by imagining two alternative mixes for raising the real level of activity up to a certain level, one of them a purely budgetary stimulus—either a tax cut or a rise in government spending, financed by borrowing from the public (so that no rise in the money supply would be involved)—and the other a purely monetary stimulus, such as an open-market purchase of bonds by the government; but with the quantities chosen being such that each of them has the same effect on the real level of activity. The monetary stimulus would operate by placing in people's hands more money than they would normally have chosen to hold at the original level of activity, as well as by making it cheaper to borrow. Buyers will therefore be correspondingly readier to offer higher prices for the goods they require; and in an imperfectly competitive world they are likely to have to do so in order to obtain these extra goods; for they will have to outbid other purchasers, who are also holding cash balances in excess of their normal requirements (at the original level of prices and incomes). Similarly, employers will be less disposed to resist wage demands (at any given level of activity) if interest rates are relatively low, and if their cash holdings are larger (and the market value of their bond holdings and other financial assets higher) than they would have chosen to hold at the original level of prices and incomes. In short, purchasers and employers will be more willing to offer higher prices and wages; whilst suppliers and wage-earners will be inclined to demand higher prices and wage rates (respectively) than in the alternative case where the same real stimulus is provided without any initial increase in people's cash balances to above their normal relationship to incomes, and without any fall in interest rates. Indeed, a purely budgetary stimulus would involve a rise in incomes and output without any rise in people's cash balances, and would thus raise interest rates; so that they will to that extent be inclined to settle for lower prices and wage rates at any level of activity than if there had been a monetary stimulus of the same order (in real terms). The process of moving to the higher level of activity will thus involve a smaller rise in the price level if it results from a budgetary stimulus than would occur under the alternative of a monetary measure.[3]

One way in which the price level may rise (at a given level of activity) as a result of a mix with a relatively expansionary monetary policy is that a relatively low rate of interest will tend to make it more profitable for people to spend a longer time searching for suitable work; for this is a form of investment, and may therefore be expected to increase as a result of a mix being chosen with relatively low rates of interest. In other words, a mix of this sort will tend to raise the 'natural' (or 'minimum sustainable') rate of unemployment. (Of course, those who do not accept the concept of a natural rate of unemployment as being a useful one can equally well describe the effect on the aggregate supply of labour without using that term.)

This concept of the 'natural' rate of unemployment—the unemployment rate at which the rate of inflation tends to rise cumulatively—is generally used to justify the view that macroeconomic measures to raise activity are virtually useless once unemployment has fallen to the 'natural' level. The present contention is, however, that the choice of a mix with a sufficiently tight monetary policy can to some extent be used to reduce the 'natural' rate of unemployment at the same time as the overall setting of policy is being directed towards reducing the *actual* rate of unemployment.[4]

For whatever reason, therefore, a mix of measures that establishes a given level of employment or of activity with a relatively high level of the money supply is likely to involve a relatively high price level. This result may be partly a case of 'thinking makes it so'. But there is probably a rational basis for this expectation. Macroeconomic theorists seem to have failed to emphasise this or to discuss it adequately—presumably in large part because they have in mind perfectly competitive models, where the price level depends only on the level of real aggregate demand and real aggregate supply, and where the actual levels of people's money holdings do not influence prices and money wage rates at any given level of activity. It has been suggested above that a more realistic picture of the real world is that the price level will be correspondingly higher (at a given level of output and activity) if the mix of macroeconomic measures is one involving a relatively high money supply (and a correspondingly lower level of government spending) than in the opposite case. It follows, therefore, that efforts to hold down the rate of interest by a relatively rapid expansion of the money supply will lead to a higher price level and, over the relevant period, a more rapid rate of inflation than if a mix of measures involving higher nominal rates of interest and higher levels of government spending had been chosen.

The lower are the rates of interest—and so the greater the supply of money with which a given level of activity (and thus a given real supply of goods and services) is established, the higher, therefore, the level of prices is likely to be. This is, of course, a separate consideration from the cost-push effect of high taxes (discussed in the preceding section), but if a mix of relatively high tax rates and relatively low interest rates is the one chosen, the price level and probably also the rate of inflation will be relatively high for both these reasons.

But businessmen are inclined to argue that high interest rates may have cost-push effects; for they feel (rightly) that if the rates of interest they have to pay are relatively high they will *want* to charge correspondingly higher prices for their products. But the prevalence of high interest rates will make it that much less likely that the prices of goods will in fact go up, as purchasers will feel less liquid—mainly as a result of the lower money supply, and the lower market prices of their financial assets.

One cannot reasonably argue that it is possible to reduce the rate of inflation by holding down interest rates through monetary policy. For that process would involve a correspondingly more rapid rate of increase in the money supply; and even those who stress the possible cost-push effects of high interest rates are not really likely to argue that a rapid increase in the money supply will be a cure for inflation. On the contrary, a tighter monetary policy (that is, a larger sale of bonds to the public) is required to accompany a cut in cost-push tax rates or a reduction in government spending (for any given level of activity) than if taxes had been higher or government spending lower. For a relatively large money supply (or a relatively rapid rate of increase in it) tends to hold up prices directly; so that a mix that involves relatively low tax rates or relatively high government spending, coupled with correspondingly greater restraint in monetary policy, is more likely to hold back inflation than is the opposite mix.

Moreover, if interest rates are kept fairly high, it will be possible (given the level of government spending) to have correspondingly lower tax rates; and the same businessmen who talk about the possible cost-push effect of high interest rates will readily acknowledge also the existence of cost-push effects from high tax rates. But if, on the other hand, interest rates are held down, tax rates will have to be correspondingly higher—so as to keep the level of activity from rising—and there will thus be more cost-push from that source. Furthermore, if there are higher tax rates on the earnings from financial assets, or on the profits from which they must be paid, this will further encourage people to move out of financial assets into goods.

One may readily grant that some of the effects of high interest rates will be in the direction of causing cost-push inflation, whilst still holding to the view that there is good reason to justify the intuitive expectation of virtually everyone that on balance it will increase the rate of inflation if money is created on a sufficiently rapid scale to hold down interest rates. One reason why increases in interest rates are less likely to have upward effects on the prices of finished products than are higher taxes is that interest rates paid by businesses are tax-deductible, whereas only *indirect* taxes paid by a business are in that category. For individuals, neither interest rate payments nor most taxes are usually deductible expenses in calculating their income tax, although in some countries the interest payments on mortgages are to some extent in that category; if they are, a rise in these interest payments is to that extent less likely to influence wage and salary demands; furthermore, high interest rates tend to hold down the price of houses, so that the average individual (at least in the long run) will not necessarily be committed to higher outgoings on his mortgage repayments as a result of a rise in interest rates, at least after the effects on the prices of newly purchased houses have had time to show themselves.

But even if a rise in interest rates had as much direct cost-push effect on the prices of the businesses paying the higher rates, and on wage demands, as did a rise in taxes paid by the businesses and wage-earners having the same effect on real demand, the other effects of the two instruments would still make the total net effect of high taxes more inflationary (at a given level of activity) than the rise in interest rates. For high taxes have also various forms of disincentive effects and various effects in reducing the real output of inherently desirable goods and services at any given level of activity, so far as they encourage the diversion of energy and manpower towards tax avoidance, tax evasion and the employment of large numbers of tax collectors and the administration of tax payments. Moreover, high interest rates tend to reduce the prices of goods directly (again, at a given level of activity) by making financial assets more attractive by comparison with the holding of real assets than they would be if interest rates were lower. If the taxes that would be raised include those on the earnings from financial assets, whereas the earnings (including capital gains and psychic returns) on real assets (such as houses) are not taxed, or not at such a high rate, again high taxes reduce the attractiveness of financial assets by comparison with those of real assets: so that a reduction in these taxes, and a corresponding increase in the return on financial assets, will tend to reduce the attractiveness of goods compared with financial assets, and so to hold down the price level at any given level of activity.

In summary, then, given the level of government spending, a government that wishes to hold down the rate of inflation will do well to secure the required restraint on private demand as far as possible by selling securities to the public rather than by high taxes.

A change of mix in the direction of lower tax rates and higher government borrowing (at any given level of activity) will probably require a bigger sale of bonds (in a given period) than the reduction of tax revenue required to offset it. For people normally change their spending as a result of a tax change to a greater extent than they are likely to change their expenditure in order to make a subscription of the same amount to government bonds. If this is so, an upward effect on real demand resulting from the tax cut would have to be offset by a larger sale of bonds, and by a corresponding fall in the money supply (if activity were to be kept constant). But this would in any case be desirable if the change of mix is to result in a fall in the price level (and, indeed, the rate of inflation)—which is what we are expecting to result from the reduction of cost-push taxes and also from the tighter monetary policy. For a fall in prices will mean that a given nominal money supply can support a higher real level of activity, and that therefore a lower nominal money supply will be needed to support the same level of activity. There is no reason why the contraction of the money supply that will occur should happen to be exactly what is required, but it will be in the right direction. The central bank will have to be prepared to take any necessary supporting monetary measures to see that the net change of the money supply is appropriate for maintaining the given level of activity in the face of the reduction in prices (compared with what they would otherwise have been) that follows the change of mix.

ARTIFICIALLY LOW INTEREST RATES

Unfortunately governments often try to hold interest rates below the level to which they would naturally rise, given the forces prevailing in the economy, and this will lead to more inflation than if nominal interest rates had been allowed to rise sooner. In periods in which high rates of inflation are expected, the level to which nominal rates of interest tend to rise appears very high by comparison with the nominal rates that most countries had been experiencing in periods of much lower rates of inflation; and this has led many people to think of nominal rates of interest in double figures as being somehow absurdly high—even when the rate of inflation is also in (or near) double figures, so that in fact the money in which the debts are being repaid is declining in real value so fast that the lender is receiving little (if any) real return on his funds, especially after tax.

If governments are reluctant to allow interest rates to rise towards the level that reflects people's expectations of inflation, then people have a strong inducement to try to move out of financial assets into real assets of one sort or another. This may push up the real level of activity, but at any given level of activity it will certainly tend to push up the price level of those existing goods, especially real estate and durable goods (including stocks of commodities), which are the closest substitutes for the long-term financial assets on which the real return has become so low; and this effect will quickly spread to the prices of newly produced goods of similar types. Eventually the unwillingness to hold financial assets at the prevailing rates of interest and with expected rates of inflation becomes so strong that governments usually have to give way and allow nominal interest rates to rise—but only after their reluctance to do so has allowed rates of inflation to go up further, and thus made the eventual level of nominal rates higher than it would have been if rates had been allowed to rise sooner.

The foregoing argument has *not* been that real interest rates—that is, nominal rates adjusted for expectations about inflation—should necessarily be raised to a higher level than they would otherwise have been (over a period of years). The deficiency of policy has been that governments have often been reluctant to allow nominal interest rates, especially those on government securities and those on bank deposits (particularly the almost universally zero nominal rates on current accounts), to rise to the levels that are appropriate, given people's expectations about the rate of inflation. As people do not usually speedily adjust their holdings of real assets and financial assets when they come to expect a higher rate of inflation, the dangers of failing to let nominal rates rise to more appropriate levels are often concealed, and it may be some time before the consequently higher rate of inflation eventuates. But as more people come to expect higher rates of inflation and to adjust their portfolios of real assets and financial assets accordingly, the price level of the real assets into which they move is inevitably pushed upwards (at any given level of activity). In order to hold down nominal rates of interest below the level to which they would otherwise naturally rise (given expectations about inflation), the government has to permit a faster rate of growth of the (nominal) money supply than would otherwise have been necessary; and this leads to increases in the price level (at each level of activity) not only of those real assets that are close substitutes for financial assets, but also that of goods and services generally. It has therefore been reluctance to let nominal rates rise that has led eventually to both inflation and nominal rates ultimately being higher than they would otherwise have been.

When the process of adjustment has taken place, the price level and (at least for a considerable period) also the rate of inflation will be higher, and nominal interest rates will also be correspondingly higher, than if nominal interest rates had been permitted to rise sooner. But a greater readiness to allow nominal interest rates (including the nominal rate on current accounts) to rise sooner would not necessarily have caused real rates of interest to be any higher—unless for a brief period. The long-run effect of trying to hold down nominal interest rates has been merely (or at least mainly) to raise the price level, and for considerable periods the rate of inflation, and with it eventually most nominal rates of interest.

Furthermore, in periods of excess demand, reluctance to let the whole structure of interest rates rise soon enough and far enough has often led eventually to greater resort to high tax rates than would otherwise have been necessary, and to consequent cost-push pressure from this source. It is true that at times it has been argued that governments have put disproportionate emphasis on monetary contraction to check booms: but very often this has been by way of direct controls over bank lending in various forms, rather than by a general rise in interest rates; and the consequent stimulus to other and less efficient forms of lending and borrowing has often reduced the efficiency of the capital market, and thus the real output of the economy, adding a further obstacle to reducing the rate of inflation at a given level of activity.

If governments had more readily allowed nominal interest rates to rise in periods of excess demand, instead of raising tax rates to such high levels, they would, then, have thereby reduced the upward pressure on prices (at any given level of activity) resulting from these high tax rates.

The negative real return on current accounts, which has become substantial as the rate of inflation has approached or reached double figures, will also have appreciable upward effects on the rate of inflation, even if rates of interest on all other financial assets are allowed to rise freely. For, in the first place, people seeking to reduce their current accounts will move instead to some extent in the direction of holding more goods, and so force the price level upwards. In the second place, so far as they move out of current accounts into interest-bearing accounts or government bonds, the rates of interest on these assets will not rise as much in nominal terms as would have occurred if the nominal rates on current accounts had risen in step with the rates on other assets. This means that as the expected rate of inflation rises, there is less inducement to people to hold financial assets generally, rather than real assets, than there would be if the rates payable on interest-bearing financial assets had risen more sharply. For both these reasons, then, the distortion of the interest rate structure that results from not paying interest on current accounts increases the attractiveness of goods compared with that of financial assets, and so raises the price level at any given level of activity.

Should the loans be long-term?

If a government is trying to improve the macroeconomic mix in a way that will tend to hold down prices, one element in the mix that is being suggested is to make available more securities in forms that will be attractive to the public. But if it succeeds in holding down inflation, and if these bonds are issued at very high nominal rates, the real returns available to their holders in future would be unexpectedly (and to the rest of the community probably unacceptably) high. One obvious way out of this is to index in some way the capital and interest on the bonds to the rate of inflation (as measured by some appropriate index). But if for some reason this is found to be unacceptable, the dimensions of the problem could be kept down by issuing the 'inflation-reducing' bonds as medium-term maturities of the order of five years; another bond issue, floated at a more appropriate nominal (and therefore real) rate could then be made if necessary when these loans matured. The gain to the lucky holders (resulting from inflation being brought under control) would thus be of only a limited duration.

If the securities issued are very short-term, the holders of them are unlikely to regard them as appreciably less liquid than money. To hold down the money supply by the issue of very short-term securities is thus likely to be little more than a piece of 'window-dressing'. It may, however, cause observers to comment favourably on the slowing down of the growth of the money supply, and there may be effects on the rate of inflation if so much attention is paid to statistics of the money supply that expectations about the rate of inflation are thereby affected. Moreover, the banks' holdings of cash ('high-powered money'), and thus their rate of lending, will be reduced if the non-bank public subscribes to even very liquid securities. But generally the issue of longer-term securities, with a significant real post-tax return on them, is likely to be the best means of operating the monetary element in the proposed package.

If index-linking is not found politically acceptable as the means of ensuring an adequate real return on long-term bonds (in a manner which, in contrast to high nominal rates, does not commit a government to paying very high nominal rates into a long-term future when the rate of inflation may have been greatly reduced), another alternative would be to issue long-term bonds at 'floating rates' (as has been done in Britain). Such bonds carry a nominal yield that is changed regularly in step with changes in the prevailing level of market-determined short-term interest rates, which may be expected to reflect current views about the probable rate of inflation. The yield on a long-term floating rate bond might be set at a predetermined percentage rate above the market rate on treasury bills.

TAX-FINANCING, BOND-FINANCING, AND GOVERNMENT SPENDING

In considering the case for shifting the mix of measures from tax-financing towards bond-financing, some account must be taken of the purpose of the government spending that is being financed. For the case for reducing tax rates is weaker when people are relatively willing to shoulder high tax rates: that is to say, when they are less likely to react to them by bidding up wage-rates and prices. Taxpayers may well find high taxes relatively acceptable if the government outlay that they consider the taxes to be financing is on items of which they strongly approve, and which they consider to be in large measure alternatives to forms of consumption that they would otherwise have had to finance themselves. On the other hand, as we have seen above (page 24), high taxes that are not widely felt to be acceptable may well give rise to higher money wage demands and higher profit claims, which can cause price rises, or even continuously higher inflation (at any given level of activity).

The risk of this occurring will depend partly on the purposes of the government expenditure and partly on the way in which it is financed. There is no reason for it to occur if the government expenditure gives rise to goods and services sold through the market at prices that reflect their costs of production; for that sort of government expenditure is to all intents and purposes like any other form of production sold through the market.

The problem arises with 'non-market expenditure' by the government; with items that are not themselves sold on the market (expenditure on social security as well as on such things as defence).[5] For the means used to restrain other potential claims on the community's resources sufficiently to leave room for the desired government spending may themselves give rise to higher income claims, and so to a higher rate of inflation at a given level of activity.

This is least likely to occur if the objects of government spending are very widely accepted as socially necessary, and as therefore justifying restraint in other forms of claim on the community's resources. An extreme form of this is in wartime, where the need to devote a very high proportion of the community's resources to defence is widely accepted, and results in a high degree of restraint in income demands and in expenditure out of any given disposable income. But government spending on defence is in other circumstances much less likely to give rise to this sort of restraint. The individual cannot reasonably regard defence spending as being an alternative to some forms of claim on the community's resources that he would have had to make out of his own pocket if the government had not undertaken it; and he is not likely in normal times to see it as a persuasive reason for him to moderate his own claims on marketable goods and services. Similarly, he may not be in sympathy with the level of outlay being made on social security payments; in particular, there has in certain countries in recent years been some evidence of resentment at the relatively generous treatment (at least compared with the past) that the unemployed, or some of them, are felt to be receiving.

But even if the objects of the government's non-market expenditure are widely accepted as desirable, an individual or a particular group or trade union, may still resent the high level of taxation that is being imposed, with the aim, as the government sees it, of holding down demand sufficiently to leave room for its own expenditure. The individual, or the particular union, is not likely to see a close association (or, indeed, any association at all) between the high marginal rate of income tax he is paying, or the high cost of beer resulting from excise duty on it, and the level of government spending on various items—even if he is completely in sympathy with the objects of government expenditure in question. Furthermore, even if the individual or group did see such a connection, they may still feel that they should do anything they can to escape or reduce their own share in the sacrifice involved in making the expenditure possible; and the more one's own disposable income is reduced in real terms, the more one is inclined to feel that one is bearing a disproportionate amount of the sacrifice involved in making possible the prevailing level of government spending—even on items that one may approve, and still more so if one believes that government spending in some forms is excessive.

In the situation of a high ratio of government taxation to total output, excessive income claims (excessive in the sense that they cannot all be satisfied without inflation with the available volume of marketable goods and services) are likely to become common. The wage and salary earner is dissatisfied with his post-tax income—or, more exactly, he is more dissatisfied with it than usual—and asks for increases in it. His employer may grant the increase and then raise the prices of his product in order to maintain his profit level. If the strong dissatisfaction with the level of the real disposable income available in the community is widespread, employers generally will be taking much the same decisions about their prices at the same time, and therefore be likely to be able to raise them without individually suffering any appreciable loss of markets. When wage settlements are centralised for the whole country these mutually inconsistent income claims are especially likely to be occurring more or less simultaneously. In successive rounds, employers and employees may then bid up prices and wages, so long as the government allows the money supply to expand sufficiently for this to be possible. If, on the other hand, the government refuses to permit monetary policy to be sufficiently accommodating, a higher level of unemployment results. The basic macroeconomic problem of stagflation therefore exists in one form or the other. Where the level of taxation and government spending is so high as to generate or encourage excessive income claims, the macroeconomic problem of stopping inflation without creating high levels of unemployment is intensified.

The particular method chosen to finance the high level of government spending may, however, have considerable effect on the intensity of the reactions of income-earners to the restraint on their real disposable incomes. They may react especially sharply to reductions in their real disposable income brought about by indirect taxes on items of mass consumption, or to high marginal income tax rates on the typical wage or salary earner.

But if the government decides to hold down the level of private demand, not by reducing the real disposable income of the individual but by offering him more attractive securities to hold, this is much less likely to lead to rising and inconsistent income demands. An individual who purchases an attractive bond reduces his consumption during the period in question less than he would as the result of a reduction of the same amount in his disposable income. The government may therefore have to sell bonds to a considerably higher value in a given period than that of the taxes that it would otherwise have had to levy if it were to achieve its desired effect through depressing consumption directly. But most of the restraint in private demand through a bond sale to the public may be brought about by diverting funds from private industry as a result of the offer of higher interest rates by the government. Naturally, this method is usually opposed by the spokesmen for industry, who see only the immediate rise in nominal interest rates that it may involve; but they do not take into account that under the alternative of higher taxation, the extra inflation generated by higher income claims is also likely to raise nominal interest rates in the longer run.

For individuals are much more likely to raise their income demands as a result of tax increases than as a result of choosing to lend more to the government when attractive securities are made available to them. In case of personal difficulty an individual can always sell government bonds; whereas if one's consumption has instead been held down as the result of the payment of taxes, one obviously cannot recover the taxes if the need for cash arises. The higher the level of government non-market expenditure, therefore, the more important it is to ensure that the means used to hold down other forms of expenditure is the issue of attractive securities, rather than high taxation. It is true that a point may eventually come (as we shall see in Chapter 5) where it is not wise to increase further the level of government borrowing from the public in view of the extra tax-push inflation that such a policy may inflict on posterity. At that point, restraint in the level of government spending and of taxation (below the level that would otherwise be desirable) could best be used to reduce the rate of inflation at any given level of activity.

Nominal and Real Rates of Interest and the Level of Taxation

At a given level of activity and a given level of government spending, if real rates of interest are relatively high, tax rates must be kept correspondingly lower—to maintain the level of activity in question. A sale of bonds by the government will raise both nominal and real rates of interest—at least initially—and so enable tax rates to be reduced. But the combined effects of the lower tax rates and the downward effect on the price level of the lower money supply and higher nominal interest rates will to some extent reduce expectations about the rate of inflation, and so the nominal interest rate. At one extreme, the real rate of interest might eventually be no higher than if the change in mix had not occurred; but, if so, taxes would have to be raised (presumably to about the same ratio to output as would have prevailed under the alternative mix), so that cost-push inflation from this source would be as great as at the outset. But in this case the raising of nominal interest in order to reduce the price level could be repeated, and so be used to have repeated downward effects on the price level. At the other extreme, real rates of interest might stay as high as the level to which they were raised initially by the change of mix, if the reduction in the price level or rate of inflation had little effect on people's expectations about the rate of inflation, and so did not lead to much subsequent downward adjustment of nominal interest rates: and in this case the downward adjustment of cost-push taxes could be permanent.

The most reasonable expectation would be that the change of mix would have some effect in reducing not only the price level, but also (at least for a time) the rate of inflation, and with it expectations about the future rate of inflation. If so, there would be some subsequent downward adjustment of nominal interest rates, and, indeed, of real interest rates—by comparison with the level prevailing just after the change of mix. But provided that real rates of interest remained somewhat above the level at which they would have been without the change of mix, tax rates could and should be somewhat lower in relation to total output than would have been possible without the change of mix; and cost-push inflation from that source would thus to that extent be lower at any given level of activity.

A Shift of Mix that Would not Raise Nominal Interest Rates

As a result of this possible effect on expectations about the rate of inflation, a shift from tax-financing to bond-financing could be consistent with some fall in nominal rates of interest. For provided that the taxes that were reduced were to some extent ones that were holding up the price level from the cost side, there would be at least a once-and-for-all fall in the price level, and a corresponding reduction in the demand for money (at any given level of real activity). This would be a factor tending to reduce nominal interest rates with a given money supply. If, therefore, bonds were sold on about the same scale as the fall in tax revenue over the period of the bond sales—so that the money supply was constant—interest rates could fall. Indeed, in order to prevent the rise in activity that would otherwise presumably be associated with the consequent rise in the real money supply (a fixed supply in nominal terms and a lower price level), the sale of bonds would have to be rather larger than the fall in tax revenue; and even if this difference equalled the fall in the demand for money at the given level of activity, nominal interest rates would not necessarily rise, especially if there were a sharp fall in the expected rate of inflation.

A government that was unwilling to adopt a mix of measures that would raise nominal interest rates might thus find that, if there were any cost-push taxes still to be reduced (or anti-cost push subsidies that it could pay), it could change its financing from taxes to borrowing without raising nominal interest rates—except perhaps very temporarily, if there were some lag before the tax reduction had its effect of reducing the price level and the expected rate of inflation at the given level of activity.

How Much Tax Cuts for How Much Bond Sales?

If a given sale of bonds has a relatively large downward effect on activity it will require a relatively large tax cut in order to offset this downward effect on demand. This means that there will be a correspondingly larger scope to reduce cost-push inflation by a reduction of the appropriate taxes. It will be helpful if a given tax reduction has relatively little effect on demand, as this means that there will be more scope to cut taxes, and so to reduce cost-push inflation, for any required stimulus to activity.

The greater is the downward impact on output of a sale of bonds the greater will be the need to offset this downward effect on activity by an appropriate tax cut. In those circumstances, where the bond sale has most of its effect on output (rather than on the price level), the scope for reducing cost-push inflation by tax reductions will therefore be correspondingly greater, in the sense that a larger real stimulus to activity by way of tax reductions will then be required.

It is true that a big tax cut (taken alone) will tend to raise the money supply, but in contrast to a rise in the money supply brought about by a purely monetary measure, a tax cut will simultaneously tend to raise the demand for money and to that extent also the rate of interest, and this will be helpful in holding down the price level through the market for goods and through the market for financial assets; whereas a purely monetary expansion will tend to a much greater extent to raise prices. Even if the net effect of the tax cut and the bond sale were to add somewhat to the money supply, the effect on activity would not be upwards; for we are ensuring that the budgetary expansion is just sufficient to offset the real contraction that would otherwise result from the monetary measures. But if the price level is to fall one would thus expect that the net effect on the money supply will have to be downwards—especially if both measures have the desired effect of reducing cost-push inflation.

In short, the proposed shift of mix towards bond-financing and away from tax-financing can work whether or not one expects budgetary measures alone to have much effect on activity. For if, on the one hand, budgetary measures have little effect on employment there is correspondingly more scope for cutting tax rates (and so cost-push inflation from that source). If, on the other hand, they have a relatively large effect on activity, whilst monetary measures have relatively slight effects on activity, a cut in the money supply by a bond sale would not produce a large downward effect on activity, so that any necessary offset to the effect on employment of a monetary contraction could be achieved with only a small tax cut. But in this situation a tightening of monetary policy would presumably be having most of its effect on the price level—rather than on output—so that the absence of scope for much reduction of cost-push inflation from the tax side would be offset by the greater scope to use monetary measures for reducing the price level. In the nature of things, therefore, one side or other of the package must provide a relatively large scope to reduce the rate of inflation. If one takes the view that monetary measures have a relatively large impact on activity, most of the effects in reducing inflation will come from the cutting of taxes; whereas if one takes the view that budgetary measures are much better able to affect activity than are monetary measures, most of the reduction in inflation will come from the monetary element in the package. But, whichever view one takes on this, the general prescription—that in order to check a rise in the price level one should tighten monetary policy and adopt an expansionary budgetary policy (preferably by tax cuts)—will achieve the desired effect.

The use of a rise in government spending to prevent the downward effect on activity that would otherwise result from the bond sales will not have the advantage of reducing cost-push inflation, unless the government spending is by way of subsidies that reduce income demands or in other ways reduce cost-push inflation. But as a rise in government spending (like a tax cut) will operate in a manner that pushes interest rates up, it will to that extent restrain the rate of inflation better than will a stimulus to activity of the same order produced by monetary means. For the lower level of the market prices of financial assets, and the lower money supply, will make people feel less liquid, and so less likely to bid up prices and money wage rates—at any given level of activity (see above page 29). A tightening of monetary policy (by bond sales, for example) offset by a rise in government spending can therefore still have the desired effect of reducing the rate of inflation; but it will require a bigger sale of bonds and a bigger rise in government spending to have the same effect in reducing the rate of inflation than if the effect on prices were obtained by a simultaneous sale of bonds and cut in (cost-push) tax rates.

Changing Both Government Spending and Government Borrowing

We have so far considered the likely effects on the price level or the rate of inflation at a given level of activity of varying both government spending and taxation; then the effect of varying taxation and government borrowing in opposite directions (whilst holding government spending constant). We shall now consider some effects of changing both the level of government spending and government borrowing without varying the level of taxation. The question we are asking is whether the aim of holding down the price level or the rate of inflation may justify a higher or lower level of both government spending and borrowing from the public than would otherwise be justified. Of course, if government spending on some item is either higher or lower than would be desirable on other grounds, the change should be made quite apart from any macroeconomic considerations.

If a government increases its spending on goods and services and simultaneously borrows from the public on a sufficient scale to keep the level of activity constant, the effect on the rate of inflation will depend to a large extent on the form taken by the rise in government spending. At one extreme, if the government merely undertook some form of production that would otherwise have been undertaken by a private firm selling it at the same price, with the same costs of production, and borrowing the same sums as the private firm would have done, there is no clear reason why the rate of inflation—or anything else of economic significance—should be affected; all that would have happened would be a change of the legal status and name of the enterprise undertaking the production.

Or if the government produced goods and services which it priced in the same way as a privately owned firm would do, and sold them in full and open competition with privately produced products, and did not use its powers of taxation or its powers to create money to finance the process, but merely operated exactly as a private firm might do, there is no reason to expect the price level to be either higher or lower than if a private firm were undertaking production with the same resources—though not necessarily of the same products. The outcome in this case need not, then, generally be different from the simplest case, where the government produces exactly the same products in the same way as a private firm would have done.

But many types of government spending give rise to the production of goods and services that are not sold to the public (such as defence, police force, diplomatic missions, salaries of administrators) or which are sold to them at less than their full cost of production (as with many health and educational services). Where this is so, it might appear that the price level will be kept down, as people are able to obtain these products without paying anything for them, or by paying something less than they would have to pay if they bought the product on the market. But many of these services (police protection and diplomatic missions, for example) would almost certainly not be purchased by the individual if they were not provided by the government; and the individual might well choose to purchase less for himself (by way of health and educational services, for example) than he uses when the government supplies them free or at low cost. Moreover, even if he would have purchased exactly the same quantity if they had been supplied at full market prices, he will have more disposable income freed for other purposes if the government supplies them below cost. The government has therefore the problem of restraining the level of expenditure on other items sufficiently to release the resources required for producing the goods and services in question. As we are here ruling out the possibility of financing the expenditure in question by taxation, or by charging for the item (at the full cost of production), or by the creation of money, the government will have to sell securities to the public at a sufficiently attractive rate to divert enough funds away from private spending, or to raise the proportion of their incomes that people save, to leave room for the extra 'non-market' expenditure that it is undertaking. It seems certain that this will involve a higher rate of interest being paid to lenders than if the government spending and borrowing under consideration had not occurred. It will also involve a lower money supply than would be required if the level of government spending (and borrowing) were lower, at the same level of total output.

So far as the price level is actually reduced, by selling a large enough volume of securities to raise nominal interest rates appreciably, the rise in government spending that is financed (or, perhaps, more than financed) by additional borrowing from the public may be seen as a way of holding down the price level at a given level of activity—as, in effect, a concealed form of subsidy. We saw in the preceding section that a better way to do this would be to reduce any cost-push taxes that exist and to substitute borrowing from the public (though only, as we shall see in Chapter 5, up to the point at which any extra cost-push inflation consequently generated for posterity as a result of any extra taxes they would then have to pay is felt to be as socially costly as the benefit to society from reducing inflation in the near future). But if we start with a society where there are no (cost-push) taxes to reduce, the sale of securities to the public, as a means of holding down the price level, would need to be offset (in its effects on activity) by a rise in government spending—which could be either on goods and services produced for the government or on subsidies.

The conclusion should be that government spending together with borrowing from the public on a sufficient scale can be employed to have some immediate downward effect on the price level; but that so long as there are cost-push taxes that could be reduced it will normally be preferable to reduce these as the sale of securities takes place, if the aim is to reduce cost-push inflation, except so far as the government spending in question is in the form of (open or concealed) subsidies that might do as much to reduce cost-push inflation as would any tax reduction.

CONCLUSION

The argument of this chapter has been that the mix of tax rates, government spending and monetary policy will have effects on the price level and so (at least during some period of time) on the rate of inflation at any given level of activity. Much more attention than in the past therefore needs to be paid to the particular mix of these measures with which a government seeks to establish a given real level of activity. This would be true even if the respective effects of the various measures on the price level and on output were in different directions from those taken to be their respective effects in the foregoing discussion.

But the relative effects, on the price level and on output, of taxation (in general), government spending (in general) and monetary policy (implemented by bond operations)are clear. Most taxes (some people would say 'all taxes') have some degree of cost-push effect; and even if one of the effects of high interest rates is also in that direction, their downward effect on demand for real assets as against financial assets, and on prices and wages directly, means that a rise in nominal interest rates has some direct downward effect on the price level, coupled with the downward effect on prices and on the expected rate of inflation that is likely to be associated with the slower growth of the money supply that the initial raising of nominal interest rates will require. Even if one granted no more than the assumption that any net cost-push effect of a rise in interest rates would be less than that of a rise in tax rates having the same effect on real demand, one would still come up with the basic policy prescription that so long as a government is concerned to reduce the rate of inflation it should reduce tax rates whenever possible and be prepared simultaneously to allow nominal interest rates to rise sufficiently to maintain the desired level of activity. If its aim is to maintain a given level of activity with less inflation it should therefore try to cut taxes and sell more bonds to the public.

The conclusion on the level of government spending must be less confident and clear-cut. In general, those forms of government spending that are wasteful, in the sense that the resources they employ would be better used in other ways, should obviously be cut; and if there are forms of government spending that can make better use of the resources these should be increased. If this prescription is followed it is likely to make the best contribution to checking inflation. But there is no general case for cutting government expenditure merely in the expectation that to do so will reduce the rate of inflation. It is true that a simultaneous cut in government spending and taxation will usually tend to reduce cost-push inflation; so that it would be true that a cut in government spending would be helpful if the only way to 'finance' it were by raising cost-push taxes. But so long as there is the alternative of government borrowing from the public, there is no presumption that a cut in government spending will necessarily reduce inflation at any given level of activity. Indeed, some forms of government spending—notably those involving, explicitly or implicitly, some form of subsidy—may be at least as effective in reducing cost-push inflation as are many forms of tax reduction.

Wherever high taxes are likely to increase the amount of inflation at any given level of activity, and where a high level of government spending does not reduce inflation (or not so much as it is increased by the high taxes) it is obvious that a low-level budget (one with low levels of both government spending and taxation) will give rise to less inflation at any given level of activity than will a high-level budget.

The most appropriate policy mix in a closed economy where the aim is to reduce the price level—and so far as possible the rate of inflation—is, then, to keep taxes low, especially those that are likely to have most cost-push effect, and to sell enough attractive financial assets to the public to keep down the growth of the money supply.

A second-best mix that would also tend to keep down the price level, but less effectively, would be to hold down both government spending and taxation; and a government that feels unable or unwilling to risk even a temporary rise in nominal interest rates could have recourse to this method. (Once the price level, and so the demand for money, is brought down by these tax cuts, this will tend to reduce nominal interest rates.)

As a third best, if it is unable and unwilling to cut taxes further, it will be likely to have some downward effect on the price level if it increases government spending (on items not financed entirely by sales at market prices) and borrows more from the public (provided this does not result in a less economic allocation of the community's resources to an extent that would offset the benefit of the downward effect on the price level resulting from the higher nominal interest rates and the lower money supply).

All these alternatives should do something to reduce the price level or the rate of inflation; whereas any other combinations of the three are far more likely to raise the price level. For a government that was worried about the more orthodox, or 'traditional', type of inflation, that with 'excess demand', the sort of mix with which demand could best be reduced would be by selling financial assets to the public, or, as a second best, reducing its own expenditure on goods and services. An increase of cost-push taxes, or a reduction in cost-reducing subsidies, would clearly be the worst way of trying to eliminate excess demand whilst simultaneously reducing the price level or the rate of inflation as quickly and as far as possible.

This amounts to saying that monetary policy should be varied with an eye to the rate of inflation, being tightened when inflation is too rapid, and being eased when it has slowed down to a tolerable rate. Simultaneously, tax rates should be cut so long as there is stagflation. Only if the rate of inflation has already fallen sufficiently to be no longer a concern would there be a case for using a rise in government spending in preference to the reduction in taxes (from the point of view of restraining price rises). Furthermore, only if it were for some reason thought impracticable to reduce taxes would it be defensible, as a second-best mix, to increase government spending on goods and services and simultaneously to sell more financial assets to the public. This amounts to saying that budgetary policy (preferably tax policy) should be varied with an eye to the level of activity so long as there is stagflation, whereas bond operations (monetary policy) should be varied with a view to holding down the rate of inflation.

4 Stopping Stagflation

The main obstacle to the restoration of the world economy to something near full employment during the years of the mid-1970s has been the fear of governments that any sort of reflationary action on their part would lead to a resumption of an intolerable rate of inflation. It is true that any sort of stimulus may raise the rate of inflation; though it is also true that in an economy where there is as much spare capacity as in many countries in the middle years of the 1970s the strong possibility exists that during the initial stages of the recovery, at least, the fall in unit costs in many industries, as they start to work closer to their most efficient level of operation, may lead to a fall in prices (or at least in the rate of inflation), especially if a large proportion of the industries in the economy determine their prices primarily by adding a mark-up to their costs. But, even in this most favourable of situations for achieving recovery without inflation, the choice of a very inflationary macroeconomic mix could lead to a rise in the price level.

We have therefore to consider the various ways of giving a short-term stimulus to the level of activity and employment, and decide which of these alternatives are likely to have the greatest upward effect on the price level, and which of them are likely to raise it least, or most likely to reduce prices.

The most 'inflationary' of the various alternatives—in the sense of having the greatest upward effect on the price level for a given real stimulus to the economy—would be the creation of money, which was then handed over to the public without their producing any goods and services in return. Picturesque, if fictional, forms of this would be dropping the money by helicopters or sending it through the post. But essentially the same mechanism is operating if the money is handed over to pensioners or any other recipients of transfer payments such as the unemployed, especially if they are among those income groups most likely to spend it. When they begin to increase their spending there will have been no increase in the goods and services available in the economy, so that there is certain to be some upward pressure on the price level at that stage; but if there is then a sharp rise in the output of goods and services (as may well happen if there are large amounts of spare resources) this upward pressure on the price level will be correspondingly less once output has risen in response to demand. (In the discussion that follows we will take this response of output to rising demand as being the same in each example, except where the method of stimulus chosen may itself affect the size of the increase in output that is forthcoming.)

A slightly different form of monetary stimulus, but probably a more common one, would be the purchase of bonds (or other financial assets) from the public by the government. The difference in this case is that the amount of bonds in the hands of the public is reduced if this alternative is chosen, so that if the supply of money in the hands of the public is the same in each case, at any given level of activity bond prices will be higher under this alternative than they would be under the first one, where no bonds were purchased from the public by the government. Under both alternatives, however, there would be some tendency for the prices of bonds and other financial assets to rise.

It is probable, but not certain, that a greater amount of money would need to be injected (to achieve a given rise in employment) by way of a bond purchase than would be required if it were used to finance a transfer payment. It is also uncertain which of these two forms of monetary stimulus would cause a bigger rise in prices. For it is true that people's total financial wealth will rise if they receive a given amount of money without selling bonds. But a bond purchase by the government will also raise the price of their remaining bond holdings; and that might do as much to stimulate their spending as the alternative form of stimulus.

The essential feature of these monetary forms of stimulus is that they operate on demand by a process that generally involves raising the prices of the goods and services demanded by the recipients of the money.

As people start to spend more freely in response to either of these forms of monetary expansion, some people who were formerly unemployed will obtain employment. If unemployment benefits have been paid to them the government's outlay in that form will fall; and this will be at least a partial offset to the rise in the money supply that started the expansion.

Furthermore, as people are absorbed into the work force they will start to pay income tax, and others already employed will pay more income-tax as their incomes increase. Employers may have to pay payroll taxes, or social security taxes, or national insurance for the additional workers they employ. Subsequently, as spending rises in the economy as an indirect consequence of the rise in employment, extra tax revenue will also be received by the government by way of indirect taxes. The greater these tax 'leakages' back to the government (and the greater the fall in social security outlays as unemployment falls) the less will be the rise in disposable incomes.

Even if there is an appreciable initial rise in disposable incomes as a result of the monetary stimulus, the extent of the ultimate rise will depend partly on how far the newly employed (or those who receive higher incomes as an indirect result of the stimulus) raise their expenditure as the result of a given rise in their disposable incomes. In particular, the unemployed may have been drawing upon accumulated savings, or borrowing, or receiving assistance from friends or relatives: and when they obtain jobs they may use substantial parts of their income to repay debts and to rebuild their accumulated savings to a more adequate level. The net increase in demand that eventually results will thus be minimised if generous unemployment benefits have been paid, and if the level of their accumulated savings on which the unemployed could draw has been high; if their disposable incomes are not much higher when employed than when they were unemployed (and in some cases of men with large families who were receiving large social services benefits when unemployed, their disposable income when they obtain jobs could actually fall); and if, when they obtain jobs, they still fear that they may lose them, and consequently seek to build up their liquid assets quickly, and to restore their credit-standing by repaying their debts.

These considerations on the demand side will be common to any form of stimulus that leads to a rise in employment. But all the forms of stimulus we have so far considered do nothing directly, 'at the first round', to add to the available supply of goods and services, so that there is almost bound to be some rise in the price level before a rise in output occurs to put more goods and services on the market. Moreover, all these monetary forms of stimulus operate by initially increasing people's financial wealth. This may be expected to increase the price level at any given level of activity, by making it necessary to offer producers higher prices and workers higher money wages in order to call forth a given level of real output. In other words, the aggregate supply curve shifts upwards, compared with its position if the same real stimulus had been given by a purely budgetary measure—such as a rise in government spending financed by borrowing from the public—which might even shift the aggregate supply schedule downwards (see Appendix 1).

This may also be true if the stimulus is provided by way of a rise in government spending on goods and services (again, assuming it to be financed by the creation of money). But one cannot say in general terms whether this form of stimulus will have a greater upward effect on the price level for a given rise in the level of employment than would a similar stimulus applied by way of a rise in transfer payments, such as pensions.

At one extreme, if the government employs people on producing goods and services—such as those for defence or government administration—that are not sold through the market, any additional consumption that is undertaken by those whose disposable incomes rise will initially face an unchanged supply of consumer goods. Some rise in the price level will usually have to occur before the required additional output of these consumer goods and services is forthcoming; and as the government will have used some of the spare capacity previously available (in order to produce the additional goods and services not sold through the market) the upward effect on the price level of consumer goods, and for that matter on that of investment goods, will be greater than if those spare resources had been left available to produce the extra consumer goods and services demanded by those whose disposable incomes have now risen. If, therefore, the rise in government spending was on goods and services not sold through the market one could expect a given initial rise in employment to cause a greater upward pressure on the prices of goods and services than if the same rise in employment had occurred by paying people to produce only those sorts of goods and services that would be in demand by consumers as employment recovered.

But it is possible for a government to produce consumer goods and services itself and sell them through the market at normal prices. One generally assumes that most government spending is not of this sort. But the government could well produce and sell those types of consumer goods and services that will be in demand as employment revives. These goods could be brought on the market almost simultaneously with the rise in consumption associated with the employment of the people who were producing them.

But generally a government—and for that matter a private firm—is likely to find it hard to assess in advance what types of goods and services will be most in demand as employment recovers. The normal course of events will therefore be for a rise in disposable incomes (whether brought about by a rise in transfer payments or in government spending on goods and services) to provide people with the means to increase their demand for various items; and, probably after some initial rise in the prices of these goods, the available supplies of them will expand. The more responsive is the supply of these products to a rise in demand for them, the less will be the ultimate rise in the price level.

If the stimulus were given by tax cuts, or by some forms of subsidies, financed by the creation of money, the effects on demand would be in some respects similar to those resulting from a rise in transfer payments such as pensions, except that if the taxes that were reduced were ones that had been having a cost-push effect (on prices or wages) a given real stimulus would be accompanied by a smaller upward effect on the price level than under the alternatives so far considered (or even by a downward pressure on prices). The extra money balances held by the beneficiaries of the tax reductions would lead them to bid up the prices of goods and services, and part of the stimulus to activity would therefore again operate through this channel. But in this case some of the stimulus could operate by reducing the costs of businesses, if taxes on their costs—payroll taxes, or excise duties on fuel they use, for example—were the ones chosen for reduction. Moreover, if there were reductions in indirect taxes or in income tax levied on typical wage-earners, and if that had some effect in reducing the rate of wage increases, this too would reduce the costs of businesses, and some of the stimulus would therefore in this case be by way of a reduction in wage costs. Of the alternatives so far considered, therefore, this is the one likely to raise the price level least, and the one having the best chance of effecting a fall in the price level.

All the forms of stimulus so far considered involve the creation of additional money. But this does not, in itself, mean that a rise in the price level must necessarily occur. As we have seen, one factor will be the extent to which output responds quickly to the rise in the demand; and if output rises simultaneously, there may be no rise in prices. Another consideration will be the extent to which the demand for money rises as incomes increase. For some rise in the money supply will be needed to meet this increased demand for it. If, however, the extra money created is more than sufficient to meet this need, there will be some tendency for prices to rise, and also for interest rates to fall, as people, finding themselves with excess cash balances, devote some of the excess to buying not only goods but also more financial assets. With any given stimulus to the real level of activity, therefore, interest rates are more likely to fall if the expansion is brought about mainly or solely by the creation of money than if it is brought about in a way that does not involve creating money (or not on such a large scale). Furthermore, for any given real expansion, those forms of stimulus that involve creating relatively large amounts of money will have correspondingly large upward effects on prices at any given level of output.

A less inflationary form of stimulus than any of those so far considered—which all involve the creation of money—would be a rise in government spending financed mainly, or wholly, by borrowing from the public. The stimulus given to activity by the rise in government spending would before long increase the output of goods and services produced; though in the short run any rise in the demand for goods and services would not be matched by additional supplies unless the goods produced for the government were of types that were in demand and were sold on the market. If additional bonds were sold to the public (in order to reduce or eliminate the upward effect on the price level that would occur if a monetary stimulus had been chosen instead) this would tend to raise nominal interest rates. The consequent rise in interest rates would to some extent hold down the price level at any given level of activity. The rise in the rate of interest would in itself probably tend also to hold down investment, and to that extent make room for other additional spending (whether in the form of extra government spending, tax concessions or additional transfer payments). But so far as investment had previously been held back by inflation, the choice of bond-financing rather than the creation of money would reduce the discouragement to those forms of investment. Furthermore, if people's expectations about the rate of inflation, and their readiness to pay higher prices and higher money wage rates, were themselves influenced by the rate of growth of the money supply, the choice of borrowing as the method of 'financing' an increase in government spending would in this sense, too, be less 'inflationary', as it would involve a smaller rise in the money supply than would any of the forms of stimulus operating through the creation of money.

The least 'inflationary' way to raise the level of activity, and the one that would be most likely to reduce the price level, would be one that operated through the reduction of cost-push taxes (or the payment of 'anti-cost-push' subsidies) and a simultaneous sale of bonds to the public. This would be the form of stimulus most likely to shift the aggregate supply schedule downwards (see Appendix 1). The tax cuts would reduce the price level (at a given level of activity). As this would reduce the demand for money at a given level of activity or employment, it would be possible simultaneously to reduce the money supply to some extent without any consequent fall in employment. If bonds were sold on a sufficient scale to reduce the money supply by something less than the percentage fall in the price level, it would therefore still leave scope for there to be some real expansion of activity. The greater the reduction in cost-push inflation that resulted from the tax cut, therefore, the larger could the sale of bonds be whilst still preserving some net stimulus to activity. Provided that additional tax cuts (or increases of subsidies) had a further downward effect on cost-push inflation, a larger tax cut, together with a larger sale of bonds, would be able to provide a correspondingly larger real stimulus than would a small tax cut (and a correspondingly small bond sale), with a constant or falling price level. The bond sales would be made in the face of a factor (a fall in the price level at or near the original level of activity) that would be tending to reduce interest rates, so that they might be made on a scale that would merely prevent this fall in interest rates from occurring. But if the relative scale of the bond sales had been such as to bring about some rise in nominal interest rates and fall in the money supply (at any given level of activity), this would be an additional factor tending to reduce the price level.

As real output rose in response to the increased level of real demand, some increase in the money supply would normally be desirable on that account, to meet the increased demand for it; and if the rise in the money supply permitted for that reason were only approximately in proportion to the rise in real output it would be broadly consistent with the stimulus not having an upward effect on prices. To that extent, therefore, the value of additional bonds sold to the public could safely be less than the reduction in tax revenue, so that part of the consequent budget deficit (in the sense of government outlay net of tax revenue) could thus be financed by the creation of money, without this having an upward effect on the price level. (Tax receipts might even rise if the tax cuts led to a very sharp rise in output.)

The sale of bonds to the public would increase the attractiveness of financial compared with real assets, and this would help to hold down the rate of inflation at any given level of activity. A rise in interest rates would at the same time have some effect in restraining those types of spending that were sensitive to increases in the rate of interest; but that would mean that there would be correspondingly more room to cut taxes, in order to keep total demand up to the required level, and so to reduce cost-push inflation arising from that source. On the other hand, so far as investment had been discouraged, and the working of the capital market impaired, by high rates of inflation, the adoption of a mix that succeeded in dampening down price increases would to that extent tend to raise the level of investment (at any given rate of interest or at any, actual or expected, level of total demand).

In summary, then, a government that wishes to have a given upward effect on the real level of employment and activity with as little upward effect on the price level as possible will concentrate the stimulus it gives upon the reduction of those taxes that it considers to be most cost-push (or upon increasing subsidies in forms that it believes reduce cost-push inflation), and will offset most or all of any upward effect that this would otherwise have on the money supply by extra sales of bonds (or other assets) to the public.

So long as there are cost-push taxes to be reduced or cost-reducing subsidies that can be paid, the taking of such measures, coupled with the borrowing of extra funds from the public, can reduce the price level at a given level of activity or make possible a higher level of activity without any rise in the price level. If the change in policy mix reduced prices by, say, 3 per cent and the demand for money at a given real level of activity by the same percentage, the adoption of the change of mix would make it possible to have the same level of activity at a lower price level if the money supply were reduced appropriately (presumably by about 3 per cent); or, alternatively, it would be possible to operate the economy at a real level of activity 3 per cent higher, with the same money supply and the same price level. By adopting a more marked change of mix along the same lines, the price level at a given level of activity could be further reduced, or a correspondingly larger real expansion could be brought about without a rise in the price level.

If, therefore, the government believes, or fears, that the very act of raising the level of activity by, say 1 per cent (relative to capacity) will raise the price level or the rate of inflation by some specified amount, it is in principle possible to change the mix of measures simultaneously in such a way as to offset the upward effect on the price level over the period in question that the more expansionary measures would otherwise be expected to bring about. The greater the extent to which a given real expansion is expected to raise the price level, therefore, the greater the change of mix that would simultaneously be required to offset it. Or, to put the same point in another way, the greater is a government's anxiety that a rise in the level of activity will push up the price level, the more important is it to give any required stimulus so far as possible by way of tax cuts, accompanied by an appropriate amount of bond sales, rather than by creating money or increasing its own level of expenditure: and the further it is willing to change its policy mix in these directions, the readier it should be to raise the level of activity towards full employment—assuming that a rise in the level of activity would normally be expected to have some upward effect on the price level.

If the government is unwilling, or feels unable, to increase its borrowing from the public it could reduce the price level by a simultaneous reduction in both government spending and cost-push taxes. Even with an unchanged money supply, the real level of activity could be increased by this combination of measures (with no consequent rise in the price level) as the result of the reduction in the price level brought about by the fall in cost-push taxes.

A much finer classification of the various policy instruments is really desirable before a government can decide which ones to vary with the aim of having as little upward effect, or as much downward effect, on prices as possible for a given real stimulus to activity. In choosing among the various taxes that a government may consider reducing (or the subsidies it may consider increasing) one obvious criterion is that a tax that has a large effect in raising business costs or in stimulating wage demands should be a prime candidate for reduction. It has to be admitted that at present we know little about the relative wage-push or cost-push effects of different taxes, and research to throw light on this matter would therefore be useful.

But even if we know little about the relative cost-push effects of different taxes, and have to assume provisionally that the reduction of revenue from one tax by a given figure will have about the same effect on cost-push or wage-push inflation as will a reduction of the revenue from another tax by the same amount, we can still say something about which taxes should be prime candidates for reduction, if we know something about the relative effects on real activity of reducing one tax rather than another by a given figure. For one tax may be paid to a greater extent than another out of what people would otherwise have saved: or, to put the point differently, the reduction of one tax by a million units of revenue may lead people to increase their spending by only very little, whereas the reduction of another may have a much bigger impact in stimulating spending for the same reduction in tax revenue. This would mean that a much bigger reduction of the first tax would be necessary to achieve the same real stimulus than if the second were chosen; if the two taxes were equally cost-push inflationary this would mean that a reduction in the first tax (the one that has *least* effect upon activity per unit of revenue) should be chosen if the aim was to achieve as much reduction as possible in cost-push inflation per unit of real stimulus to activity. It is true that the choice of this tax as the prime candidate for reduction would imply that there would be a larger rise in the money supply (other things equal) for a given stimulus to activity; and that these monetary effects might have to be offset, therefore, by a correspondingly larger sale of bonds than would be required if the other tax were reduced. It could thus be ensured that the real stimulus to activity was the same under both alternatives, but that the tax reduction was concentrated on those taxes that gave least stimulus to activity—in order that the maximum of reduction in tax-push could be achieved for a given stimulus.

Of course, if we have enough knowledge of the relative cost-push effects of different taxes and also of their respective effects on activity per unit of revenue, these different considerations would have to be weighed together. If it happened that the most cost-push taxes were those that had relatively little effect on activity the two criteria would both point to the same candidate for reduction: but if the most cost-push taxes happened to be those that had the most effect on the real level of demand (per unit of revenue) these two considerations would be conflicting, and some method of weighing the size of these different effects against one another would therefore be desirable.

As the most cost-push taxes were reduced or eliminated there would obviously be less of a case for providing a further stimulus in this way; it might then be desirable at this, or indeed at any, stage to decide whether the payment of some form of generalised subsidy on business costs or on wages would be a preferable way of reducing cost-push and wage-push inflation.

There might also be a further criterion to be borne in mind. Some taxes may have an especially strong disincentive effect, by reducing people's willingness to work hard or efficiently or to seek work. These may or may not also be those forms of taxes that encourage high wage demands or tend to raise cost-based prices most strongly. But any taxes that tend to a marked extent to discourage effort, or impair the allocation of resources, or divert manpower and effort towards the collection, administration, avoidance and evasion of taxes, tend to raise the price level at any given level of money incomes or activity; so that this aspect too would need to be borne in mind.

VARYING THE MIX IN THE COURSE OF A RECOVERY

When there are considerable amounts of unused resources in an economy it should be possible to generate recovery with a minimal upward effect on the price level in the short run, as considerable increases in productivity should occur while activity is recovering. On the other hand, some opponents of the provision of a short, sharp stimulus to recovery have argued that it will take time for extra real output to be produced, and still more time for investment to take place in those areas where there are bottlenecks. One may therefore, according to the relative stress one places on each of these considerations, come up with different views as to whether most of the stimulus to recovery should be introduced early in the recovery (a 'front-loaded' recovery) or whether the major measures of stimulation should come later (a 'back-loaded' recovery).

But whatever view one wishes to take on this matter, it should be possible to vary the mix of macroeconomic measures over the course of the recovery in order to reflect one's judgment on this point. If it is indeed true—as the writer would believe to be the most likely situation—that when there are large amounts of spare resources the risk of high or rising rates of inflation is less than in later stages of the recovery, a twist of the macroeconomic mix in a less inflationary direction (lower tax rates and higher interest rates) would be most useful later in the recovery, when bottlenecks are starting to appear. On the other hand, if there are good grounds for fears of higher rates of inflation in the earlier stages (on the basis of the view that it takes time for industry to produce extra output to meet a sudden revival of demand, even when there are ample spare resources), then a switch towards a less inflationary mix, of lower tax rates and higher interest rates, rather than the reverse, may be appropriate at that earlier stage of the recovery. But whatever the view one takes as to the way in which the risk of inflation will change over the period of the recovery, a corresponding offsetting variation of the macroeconomic mix over the same period could be made to counter it. Moreover, a temporary change of mix of this sort would, by definition, be one that would require to be reversed in another phase of the recovery, so that it would not be one that could be criticised as in some way being likely to present any lasting problems. Furthermore, the knowledge that a switch of the mix in an appropriate direction at the right moment could offset the upward effect on the rate of inflation that might be expected to result from raising the economy closer to the level of full employment should make governments readier to take stimulatory measures, so far as they are inhibited from doing so by fears of an early increase in the rate of inflation; and the knowledge that they can switch to a less inflationary mix, if necessary, at a later stage of the recovery should prevent them from being too fearful that the recovery may raise the rate of inflation in its later stages. They should therefore plan for the overall effect of their measures of stimulation to be, in real terms, appropriate to the level of unutilised resources in the economy, and simultaneously plan to change the mix of macroeconomic measures during the recovery in such a way that it will have an anti-inflationary twist at those stages of the recovery where the risk of a rapid rise in the price level is felt to be greatest.

CAN A BUDGETARY EXPANSION CONTINUE IN THE LONG RUN?

In the very long run some forms of budgetary expansion may cease to be effective. For example, if there were a rise in government spending and a tax increase of the same order, any upward effect on incomes (through the 'balanced budget multiplier') would gradually dwindle in the face of a fixed money supply—at least according to the usual analysis—even apart from the cost-push effects of the taxes. For when incomes are at a higher level in relation to the money supply than people feel to be normal—so the argument goes—they will start to save a higher proportion of their incomes, in order to rebuild their holdings of money (and also of liquid assets generally, including bonds) to a more normal relationship to their incomes. This will tend to pull down the level of national income until it is restored to its normal relationship to the money supply, which we have assumed to be kept fixed.

The same sort of argument can be made about the eventual expiration of a stimulus that is brought about through an expansion in the money supply. The consequent fall in the rate of interest will at first stimulate activity, but people will then find that as prices rise—or as expectations about the rate of inflation rise—their money balances are inadequate, and they will therefore try to rebuild them by saving more at each income level; and in the process they will reduce the level of real income and output, so that the ultimate effect of the rise in the money supply will be entirely, or almost entirely, on the price level, rather than on real output. The 'monetarist' view would be that the real upward effect on activity exhausts itself in a fairly short time; the 'non-monetarist' or so-called 'Keynesian' view would be that it takes so long to exhaust itself that this weakening of its effect is not really a relevant consideration for the formulation of macroeconomic policy. But there is now sufficient agreement among most 'monetarists' and 'non-monetarists' about the underlying theory for it to be possible to say that, '. . . we are now all Keynesians in the short run, those of us who are not dead in the long run are at least near-monetarists'.[1]

But this analysis of the possible exhaustion of either a monetary or budgetary stimulus takes no account of the possibility that some policy mixes through which an expansion may be brought about can have at any rate a once-and-for-all but lasting upward effect on activity, because they have a downward effect on the price level at any given level of activity. If a budgetary expansion is brought about by a cut in taxes coupled with an equal sale of bonds, some fall in the price level can be expected, especially if some of the taxes cut are ones that are tending to raise costs or wages at the prevailing level of activity. The consequent rise in the *real* money supply (the lower price level coupled with the fixed nominal supply) will therefore make it possible to support a higher real level of activity, whilst still leaving the money supply in nominal terms at or above its normal relationship to the level of nominal incomes. There is therefore no reason whatever to suppose that this initial stimulus will be eventually reversed. For the reversal that orthodox theory expects comes about essentially because the analysis appears either to assume implicitly that taxes cannot have a cost-push effect, or else that the stimulus does not take the form of reducing any of those taxes, nor of paying subsidies of a cost-reducing nature.

Furthermore, even if this form of stimulus is one that causes some rise in the price level, although there will then not be so much rise in the real level of activity as would otherwise be possible with a given supply of money, it also means that nominal rates of interest will tend to rise. This will have a helpful effect. For, as we have seen, a rise in nominal rates of interest will have some effect in the direction of holding down the price level: and, secondly, the slower rate of increase in the money supply (compared with a monetary stimulus) may also be expected to hold down the price level at any given level of activity.

If, therefore, the mix of measures with which a stimulus is given is mainly budgetary, so that it keeps up interest rates at any given level of activity, this will have some effect in the direction of reducing the price level at each level of activity, and so will bring about a once-and-for-all (but lasting) increase in the real money supply without a change in the nominal money supply.

Furthermore, if the stimulus is given by a cut in cost-push taxes (or by the payment of cost-reducing subsidies) coupled with a simultaneous sale of bonds, the consequent reduction in the price level, both through the reduction of tax-push and through the effects on the price level of the bond sales, will for these various reasons enable a given nominal money supply to support a higher real level of output.

By contrast, if a government tries to give the stimulus by increasing equally both taxes and government spending—through the 'balanced budget multiplier'—the consequent increase in cost-push inflation may prevent there being any stimulus. For without a rise in the money supply, people will feel their money balances are inadequate in the light of the higher price level resulting from the cost-push taxes, and will therefore save a higher proportion of their incomes until these have been rebuilt, and until the value of national income has been reduced to its normal relationship to the fixed money supply. Indeed, so long as cost-push tax rates remain above their original level, the level of activity may be dragged down further, in real terms, so that it ends up lower than it would have been without the stimulus; for the price level will be higher (at any given real level of activity) as a result of the increase in cost-push taxes.

If, however, the stimulus is given by way of a rise in the government's spending on goods and services and a simultaneous sale of bonds, there will be some rise in rates of interest at any given level of activity as a result of the bond sale coupled with the higher level of activity; and the consequent downward movement in the price level will make it possible for the fixed nominal money supply to support a higher level of real income. The higher rate of interest will also encourage people to make some economies in their holdings of cash balances, so that a given money supply will consequently be able to support a higher level of income or output. There will therefore not be any reason to expect that a stimulus given in this way will be subsequently negated, provided that it has some downward effect on the price level at a given level of activity. But this is likely to necessitate a reduction in the money supply—that is, a sale of bonds greater than the rise in government spending. As the rise in interest rates will induce some economising in cash balances (in relation to income) it will still be possible for income to rise, despite the fall in the money supply; and the higher yield on financial assets, together with the fall in the money supply, may be expected to have some direct downward effect on the price level of goods at any given level of activity.

A once-and-for-all, but lasting, non-inflationary stimulus can thus be given by this form of expansion through increased government spending plus bond sales. There may well be still greater scope for giving such a stimulus by the method of cutting cost-push taxes and simultaneously increasing bond sales. This contrasts with the probability that the forms of stimulus given mainly by monetary means, or one that is given by means of simultaneous increases in government spending and taxation, are far more likely to be of diminishing effect as time goes on, and that the stimulus they can give to the real level of activity may eventually vanish, at least in the longer run.

The case for providing a stimulus by means of a mix that is less likely to be inflationary—perferably one involving tax cuts and bond sales—is, therefore, not only that inflation is best avoided, but also that a stimulus provided in this way is not likely to carry the seeds of its own undoing.

But if a form of stimulus is chosen that has a considerable upward effect on the price level, this may well lead to higher wage demands, and greater readiness on the part of businesses to grant them, than if some less inflationary means had been chosen to provide the same real stimulus. If money wage rates increase sharply, the effect of the real stimulus could consequently be considerably reduced, or even eliminated or reversed; for if the rise in prices is the main channel through which businesses are being induced to produce more, a substantial rise in wage costs will obviously reduce or even eliminate this inducement to businesses to increase output. If, however, the stimulus chosen is one that tends to hold the rate of inflation constant or even to reduce it, it is more likely that wage increases will be dampened, and to that extent the efficacy of a given initial stimulus would be the greater.

The choice of one of the least inflationary forms of stimulus to activity is therefore desirable not only if the government also wishes to restrain inflation, but also because the real effect of the measures will therefore be more likely to continue; both because it will then be less likely that this form of stimulus will result in higher money wage rates, and also because (as we saw above) this is less likely to lead people to save a higher proportion of their incomes (with a view to rebuilding the real level of their reserves of financial assets) than is a monetary stimulus.

Even if neither of these repercussions, taken alone, fully offsets the stimulus given by a more inflationary type of mix, there is clearly a much greater likelihood that this will be the combined effect of both these repercussions taken together.

BELIEF IN THE 'PHILLIPS CURVE' AND THE POLICY MIX

Whatever the views of economists, governments continue to act as if they believed there was some relationship between the level of activity (or unemployment) and the rate of inflation. This relationship—which we may loosely call a 'Phillips curve'—implies that if the aim is to reduce the rate of inflation a higher level of unemployment may have to be accepted, though some would argue that this will be necessary only temporarily, while expectations about inflation are being changed, so that the curve is correspondingly shifted. Whether or not there is in this sense in fact a 'tradeoff' between unemployment and inflation, the belief in the existence of such a tradeoff continues to exist in the minds of many policy-makers, and this has important implications for policy. We have now to ask about the relationship between the policy prescriptions that governments derive from this assumed relationship and the prescriptions about the policy mix outlined above.

There are logically four possibilities:

1. That a rise in unemployment will not reduce inflation, and that governments *know* it will not; so that they therefore aim at keeping their economies as close as possible to full employment, believing that this will not increase the rate of inflation;
2. A rise in unemployment may *not really* reduce inflation, but governments may *believe* it will; if so, they will operate their economies at less than full employment in the hope of thereby reducing the rate of inflation, even though they have in fact nothing to gain by way of reduced inflation through sacrifice of potential output;
3. Higher unemployment may *in fact* reduce inflation, but governments may not *believe* that it will, so that they will operate their economies at full employment (or as near to full employment as they can manage), even though that makes the rate of inflation higher than it would otherwise have been, and higher than they would have chosen if they had realised that there was a tradeoff;
4. Finally, it is possible that higher unemployment will reduce inflation *and governments know that it will*, and that they therefore decide to accept a higher level of unemployment in order to secure a lower rate of inflation—though this means also a lower level of real output than would otherwise be possible.

Let us consider the proposed policy mix in the context of each of these four possibilities. First, if high unemployment does not reduce inflation, and the government knows this to be so, it must and should concentrate on achieving the least inflationary policy mix at 'full employment' (which is the only sensible level at which to operate the economy if there is no 'Phillips' relationship). In this case, the policy mix is all-important, in the sense that there is no point in trying to find an optimal combination of unemployment and inflation, as none exists.

It will therefore be desirable (in this case as in the others) for the government to try to reduce cost-push taxation, either by curbing also its own spending on goods and services, or by shifting towards borrowing from the public. But there will not be so much to gain in this first case (as there will be in the others), by shifting the policy mix towards reducing taxation and borrowing more from the public; for the achievement of a more appropriate ('less inflationary') policy mix will not, in this case, enable the government to operate the economy at a higher level of activity than would be possible without that policy mix (for it will presumably be trying to maintain the economy at full employment in any event). A shift of mix in the suggested directions will, however, bring the benefit of less inflation and a better allocation of resources at a given level of activity than if the mix were a more inflationary one.

In our second case—where the government operates the economy at less than full employment in the mistaken hope of reducing the rate of inflation—the adoption of a less inflationary policy mix will reduce the rate of inflation at any given level of activity, and therefore presumably make the government less inclined to accept the loss of output in the (vain) hope of bringing the rate of inflation down. The social benefits of reducing the rate of inflation by adopting a more appropriate policy mix will thus in this case be greater than in the first case we considered, because the government will feel able to operate the economy at nearer to full employment as a result of adopting a less inflationary policy mix. Furthermore, in this case it will not increase the rate of inflation if it allows the economy to operate at nearer to full employment.

In the third case—where higher unemployment reduces inflation, but the government does not believe that this is so—the government will presumably be operating the economy at full employment and will therefore be permitting a higher rate of inflation than would occur if the economy were operated at a lower level of activity. The adoption of a less inflationary (and thus more appropriate) policy mix will in this case reduce the rate of inflation at full employment, and so reduce also the social costs associated with keeping activity at such a high level. The shift towards bond-financing (or lower government spending) and lower taxes will be worth taking further under this alternative, because the continued downward effect on the rate of inflation brought about by such a shift may be especially desirable, as there will be much to gain from reducing the high rate of inflation, which will presumably be inflicting high social costs as a result of trying to operate the economy at full employment. The more 'pigheaded' a government is about trying to maintain full employment in a country where unemployment could reduce inflation, the more important is it to reduce the rate of inflation by other means.

Finally, in the fourth case, where high unemployment can reduce inflation, and the government knows this to be so, the scope for social gain by shifting the policy mix in the suggested direction is greatest, for such a shift offers a hope of getting down the rate of inflation by a means other than operating the economy at less than full employment, or at least of 'shifting the Phillips curve', so that a given rate of inflation is consistent with a lower rate of unemployment (or so that a lower rate of inflation is consistent with a given rate of unemployment). In this case, a shift of the mix in the appropriate direction will make governments able and willing to achieve the social benefits of a rise in the available output of real goods and services by using a less inflationary mix (rather than by operating at less than full employment) to achieve a given reduction in the rate of inflation.

To sum up, then, whether there is or is not a Phillips curve, and whether or not governments act on the assumption that there is one, a change in the policy mix in the direction of bond-financing rather than tax-financing, or of lower government spending on goods and services together with a reduction in cost-push taxation, can help to bring down the rate of inflation. In addition, if the government acts in the belief that there is a Phillips curve (whether there is one or not), the adoption of a more appropriate policy mix can bring the additional benefit of enabling the government to operate the economy at a higher level of activity for any given rate of inflation than would be possible with a more inflationary policy mix. If the government is determined to operate the economy at full employment, and does so whatever policy mix it adopts, the shift of the mix in a less inflationary direction will reduce the rate of inflation associated with the level of activity in question, and so the social costs imposed on the country by a high rate of inflation.

Even if a government is so convinced of the existence of a Phillips curve that it holds down the level of activity to below full employment irrespective of the scope that exists for adopting a less inflationary policy mix, a shift of the mix of its macro-measures in the suggested directions will reduce the social costs associated with that level of unemployment, to the extent that it reduces the rate of inflation. It will thus be preferable for the government to achieve the lower level of demand at which it is aiming by means that reduce taxes as far as possible, and to offset any undesired upward effect on activity of the tax cuts by selling more bonds to the public. For if, on the other hand, it refrains from reducing taxes, on the assumption that a tax reduction will inevitably be 'inflationary' (in some sense), the expectation must be that there will in fact consequently be more inflation than if it reduced taxes and tightened monetary policy. For so long as tax rates have any upward (cost-push) effect on the rate of inflation or the price level, or so long as any sale of bonds and the consequent rise in interest rates and slower rise in the money supply will have some direct downward effect on the price level, a shift of the policy mix towards lower taxes and greater bond sales will always have some downward effect on the price level at the chosen level of activity. Even a rise in government spending whose effects on the money supply are offset by bond sales would have some effect in reducing the price level (at the given level of activity), so long as a rise in interest rates has some downward effect on the price level.

Is the Concept of a Phillips Curve Still Valid?

For these reasons, the rate of inflation at any given level of activity will vary according to the mix of measures with which that level of activity is established. One could have price stability and full employment if tax rates were low enough (with correspondingly greater bond sales or lower government spending). Or one could have mass unemployment and hyperinflation if one created money fast enough whilst simultaneously raising tax rates to very high levels. In this sense there can be little left of the idea of a Phillips curve. One might try to rescue it by assuming, in some sense, that the macroeconomic mix was held constant as one moved from one level of activity to a higher (or lower) one. But would this mean that taxes and government spending were at the same ratio to total output? And what would it mean about bond sales? Clearly any such assumptions must be purely arbitrary. It is better to concentrate on the mix and forget the Phillips curve.

In any case, the evidence about the continued existence of a Phillips curve is at best debatable (even if we are willing to accept that something like it existed in the past). The adjustments to expectations that have during the 1970s apparently shifted the position of any curve there may be, depend mainly on people's experience of rates of inflation in the fairly recent past; so that any measures of policy we can adopt to reduce the price level, and so the rate of inflation for some period, will presumably shift whatever relationship there may be. At any rate, during the mid-1970s, when levels of unemployment have been at much higher rates than any experienced before in the years since the Second World War, it is a bold government that is prepared to gamble on the hope that a small rise in unemployment at such levels as these will have any effect in reducing inflation; so that the tail-end of the curve may well have disappeared, even if the body of it still has some substance. In any case, the expectations seem in recent years to have virtually swallowed up any curve there might be. They may well have been at one time merely the grin on the cat, but the cat itself seems to have gradually faded, leaving little but the grin. We ought now to concentrate on wiping out the grin—at least until such time as we have convincing evidence that there really is a cat there.

> . . . it vanished quite slowly, beginning with the end of the tail, and ending with the grin, which remained some time after the rest of it had gone (Lewis Carroll, *Alice's Adventures in Wonderland*, Chapter 6.)

The 'Expectations-adjusted' Phillips Curve

The version of the Phillips relationship that has received widest currency in the literature in recent years, and which has apparently most influenced policy in the mid-1970s, is that in which the curve is adjusted for expectations about inflation. This view interprets the curve as providing only a temporary 'tradeoff' between unemployment and inflation. For if a government provides a stimulus to activity that raises the rate of inflation, the stimulus will last only until expectations about inflation have been fully adjusted upwards to the actual rate; money wages will then rise to an extent that will eliminate the stimulus to employment. This view also argues that a rise in unemployment above its 'natural' or 'minimum sustainable' level will be necessary in order to reduce the rate of inflation.

It may well have been true in the past that governments have usually tried to reduce unemployment by using some mix of measures that raised the rate of inflation. But this does not prove or imply that such a mix need always be chosen. A stimulus provided by cutting cost-push taxes (coupled with an appropriate amount of bond sales) is much less likely to raise the rate of inflation and may even reduce it. Moreover, if a change of mix can reduce the rate of inflation, it is correspondingly less necessary to accept a rate of unemployment that is, temporarily, unusually high, merely in order to reduce the rate of inflation. Furthermore, the adoption of a less inflationary mix can, as we have seen, reduce the 'natural' rate of unemployment (the rate at which inflation tends to increase)—so far as there is a useful meaning attaching to this concept.

COULD RELATIVELY LOW INTEREST RATES ACTUALLY DEPRESS ACTIVITY?

In all the discussion up to now we have made the orthodox assumption that a rise in interest rates will tend to depress the level of activity. We have seen that a mix involving relatively low interest rates will tend to cause more upward pressure on prices at a given level of activity than will alternative mixes (especially ones involving lower cost-push taxes). But it has not been argued that full employment is impossible if we adopt the 'wrong' sort of mix; for even with high taxes and very low real interest rates it may well be possible to restore or maintain full employment (provided that the government and those who elect it are prepared to tolerate very high rates of inflation in order to do so), so long as the general level of demand reacts in the normally expected way to a change in interest rates.

But a very much more serious situation would result from the adoption of the wrong sort of mix if the decision to keep interest rates (at least, real interest rates) relatively low actually tended to depress activity. Most of us would probably feel this possibility to be too remote to be worth considering; for the expectation that a reduction in interest rates normally stimulates activity is deeply ingrained in our way of thinking. It is true that some people take the view that investment is generally rather insensitive to changes in interest rates (especially in a recession); but there would be widespread agreement that, so far as they do react to interest rates, investment decisions—that is, decisions to increase the real stock of capital—will be affected in an upward direction if interest rates fall. It appears, however, that there are some types of investment that may actually be likely to rise when interest rates increase, though we do not know how important such types of investment are in total investment.[2]

It is, however, hard to believe that such forms of investment are important enough for total investment to react in this way to a change in interest rates. But it is much easier to accept that total investment may be rather insensitive to interest changes (as some investigations have suggested); and this insensitiveness may be greater in periods of rapid inflation. For great uncertainty about future rates of inflation makes it hard or impossible for lenders to decide what premium they should insist on receiving (above the interest rates they would otherwise demand) to cover the uncertainty about future changes in the value of money, whilst borrowers are equally uncertain about what sort of premium it is worth their while to pay. This may mean that small changes of interest rates in either direction will not do much to bring borrowers and lenders closer together, or to affect investment plans.

If total investment reacts relatively little to changes in interest rates, the main part of the effect on total demand of a change in interest rates depends, therefore, on how people's consumption may be influenced by it. There is nothing new about suggesting that the proportion of people's income that they choose to save may be influenced either upwards or downwards by a fall in the rate of interest. If people save with the aim of providing themselves with sufficient earning assets to yield a more or less fixed income when they retire, or against the risk of becoming unemployed ('hump saving' or 'target saving', as it has been called), then if the yield on their earning assets is relatively low, they will presumably be more willing to sacrifice current consumption in order to build up their stock of such assets. For this sort of saving, therefore, a rise in interest rates may well tend to reduce the proportion of income saved, rather than to increase it.[3]

It may be especially true that in recent years, as people have become aware of the effects of inflation in causing a fall in the real value of their assets, and of how far the real return that these assets are yielding has fallen as real post-tax interest rates have declined, they may have become more inclined to increase the proportion of their incomes saved than they would have been if the real rate of return on their financial assets had been higher. As interest rates (especially after tax) have in many countries not kept pace with people's expectations about the future rate of inflation, the real rate of interest, in this relevant sense, has been low or even negative; and this may well have been one of the factors in bringing about the very marked rise in the proportion of disposable incomes saved in many countries in the mid-1970s. If the propensity to save is in fact liable to rise sharply, partly as a result of the real return on financial assets being held down, the resulting fall in consumption (at any given level of activity) could outweigh any upward effect there might be on investment as a result of maintaining interest rates at a relatively low level. In this case, then, the choice of a mix with relatively low interest rates, with the aim of thereby providing a stimulus to activity, could actually depress employment further.

If this situation occurs in reality, therefore, the adoption of the wrong sort of mix could thus be much more disastrously stagflationary than it would be on the orthodox assumption that total demand rises when interest rates fall. One must not lay oneself open to the charge of adopting 'scare tactics' by exaggerating the risk that total demand might react in this perverse way to changes in interest rates; but the possibility is clearly not so farfetched that it can safely be left out of account in choosing the appropriate macroeconomic mix. Moreover, if the consequence of keeping real interest rates too low is that both unemployment and inflation remain higher than governments intend and expect, it would help to explain the widespread continuance of stagflation, so far as governments have been trying to correct recessions by a mix of measures that failed to raise interest rates soon enough and far enough.

For if demand tends to fall when interest rates are kept relatively low in real terms, this will mean that every attempt by a government to raise activity by holding down interest rates actually works in the direction of increasing unemployment; and even the failure of a government to allow nominal interest rates to rise fully in step with people's expectations about the rate of inflation would in this sense constitute a reduction in interest rates. The adoption of an 'inflationary' type of policy mix of this sort will therefore tend to drive the economy further towards stagflation; for not only will it tend to raise unemployment, but the relatively rapid rise in the money supply (compared with a situation where monetary policy had been used in such a way as to let interest rates increase) will place some additional upward pressure on the price level at any given level of activity.

But, fortunately, if we apply the principles that have been suggested above as appropriate in a situation of stagflation—on the orthodox assumptions about the response of the level of demand to changes in interest rates—the best types of mix will also be appropriate if the economy reacts in this unexpected (and presumably unusual) way to a change in interest rates. For it will also be true in this case that budgetary measures of expansion (preferably the reduction of cost-push taxes) will raise the level of activity. Indeed, their effectiveness will be rather greater if the rise in interest rates that occurs (with a fixed, or only slowly expanding, money supply) when budgetary measures of expansion are employed has the effect of further stimulating demand, in contrast to the dampening of activity that would result on the normal assumption about the effects of a rise in interest rates.

Furthermore, the tightening of monetary policy, which has been recommended above as the appropriate means for holding down the price level, would, if used in a situation of stagflation, tend both to check inflation and to reduce unemployment in an economy where demand rose as interest rates were increased. In other words, a tight monetary policy would become the ideal weapon for dealing with stagflation in both its aspects. For it would tend not only to raise activity, but it would also tend to hold down the price level at each level of activity below what it would otherwise have been, by restraining the rise in the money supply.

In short, if it should happen that the level of demand is actually stimulated by a rise in interest rates, the adoption of a policy that holds real interest rates down will make stagflation worse on both scores. (One can, perhaps, see this tendency at work in those countries that have not permitted interest rates to rise as rapidly as people's expectations about the rate of inflation.) By the same token, therefore, a tightening of monetary policy would in these circumstances attack both of the horns of the stagflationary dilemma; for it would both stimulate activity and help to hold down the price level.

But we do not at present know enough about the reaction of demand to changes in interest rates to be confident that the use of a tight monetary policy alone will both check inflation and raise activity. We should therefore adhere to the application of both aspects of the policy mix suggested above; and this includes the use of expansionary budgetary measures (preferably the reduction of cost-push taxes) to overcome unemployment. If we find that the simultaneous adoption of a tight monetary policy (that is, bond sales by the government) helps to stimulate activity, as well as to check price increases, it will simply mean that we do not require to provide as much budgetary stimulus as would otherwise have been required.

Actual Policies Contrasted with the Proposed Mix

The actual policies pursued by governments in stagflationary conditions have been in marked contrast to those proposed above. In general, governments have been reluctant to reduce tax rates, even though they are increasingly aware of their cost-push and wage-push effects. They are inclined to argue that tax cuts will raise the rate of increase in the money supply, and so the rate of inflation. Taken by itself, this conclusion would generally be correct; but the aim should be simultaneously to reduce tax rates and sell bonds, so that there will be, temporarily at least, a rise in the real post-tax interest rates received by the lender.

At the same time, governments are reluctant to bring about the rise in rates of interest that would be necessary to give the lender attractive returns, partly because they fear the political repercussions by way of the votes of mortgage-payers, and because they fear that a rise in rates of interest would hold down down the level of building activity and private investment. Again, if the rise in interest rates were the only measure advocated, that analysis would be correct. But if, on the other hand, rates of interest are held down, tax rates will also have to be kept correspondingly higher, or government spending curtailed. To put the same point differently, so far as a rise in interest rates would check desirable forms of investment (building, for instance), it would be both feasible and desirable simultaneously to give an equal or greater stimulus to that form of investment by some tax concessions or subsidies, or by direct government spending on the items in question.

The real danger is that fears that tax concessions will generate a rise in the money supply may lead governments to keep tax rates high and activity correspondingly low. As this also keeps tax receipts down and unemployment payments up, the government becomes correspondingly more concerned about the state of the 'public sector borrowing requirement' or 'budget deficit', and may consequently be tempted to raise tax rates still further, and so have a still bigger downward impact on activity and a further upward impact on tax-push inflation. At the same time, governments do not usually make full use of the scope that exists for holding down the price level (at any given level of activity) through the sale of bonds, by way of the repercussions of bond sales upon prices in the markets for real and financial assets, and through the consequently slower rate of increase in the money supply.

Electorally, the strongest pressures on governments are in the direction of opposing increases in interest rates. They come from those businesses that will have to pay the higher rates; from some financial institutions that are primarily concerned about the downward effect that a rise in nominal interest rates would have upon the market value of their assets; and from those who have to repay mortgages: and these groups are far better organised to express their views than are the countless savers and lenders who suffer from inflation, and the unemployed who would prefer to have jobs. The whole country suffers from the stagflation, but the greatest suffering is inflicted on those least organised to oppose it. Even if they realised that their interests are that there should be a stimulus to activity provided as far as possible by means of tax cuts and as little as possible (if at all) by reducing rates of interest, they would not be well organised to express this point of view. The best prospect of an enlightened form of expansionary macroeconomic policy(with an appropriate mix) being adopted, is, therefore, if the principal spokesmen in other groups—especially the policy advisers, the business economists, academics, trade union leaders and journalists—come to realise the nature of the sorts of macroeconomic mix that are most likely to bring about recovery without inflation.

CONCLUSION

In summary, then, the right policy mix for overcoming stagflation is to cut cost-push taxes (or pay anti-cost-push subsidies) until full employment is restored, whilst selling bonds, and allowing post-tax real interest rates to rise until inflation is stopped. But this would be consistent, in some circumstances, with an actual fall in nominal interest rates.[4]

5 Problems, Objections and Complications

In the two previous chapters we have considered alternative combinations of monetary and budgetary measures, with a view to deciding what sorts of combinations are most likely to enable an economy to minimise the rate of inflation, or at least the upward pressure on the price level, at a given level of activity; and also the type of mix that is most likely to raise activity with as little risk as possible of raising the price level.

In the present chapter we will consider some real and imagined difficulties that there may be in the way of adopting such policies: and consider some social costs that might arise if the change of mix were carried too far.

'MOST OF THE UNEMPLOYMENT IS STRUCTURAL'

Some people may be inclined to oppose efforts to secure a more appropriate policy mix on the—strictly speaking, irrelevant—grounds that there are more urgently needed policy measures. In particular, some may point to the problems posed by 'structural' unemployment, and to the need to retrain and resettle people so as to make them better fitted to fill the positions where they are really needed.

It should therefore be stressed that nothing in the proposals made in this book is in any way intended to argue against such measures as these. Most of those who believe that a very high proportion of recent levels of unemployment has been due to 'structural' factors would presumably agree that a significant amount of the unemployment has nevertheless been due to the fact that output has been held down by the macroeconomic policies adopted. Moreover, if the adoption of a less inflationary mix of macroeconomic measures enables a higher level of activity to be established, it will make it easier to see where there are jobs that need filling, and therefore what sorts of retraining and resettling of existing manpower are required; and the manpower, when retrained, will then be more readily absorbed. Furthermore, an unduly high level of unemployment makes people especially unwilling to make the effort to find work and to retrain, as their efforts to find jobs are thus so often met with frustration, whilst businesses are less willing to retrain people; and governments that believe that holding down government spending is at least part of the cure for inflation are not likely to spend as much as would probably be desirable on the various forms of retraining of manpower and other policies for overcoming structural difficulties. The solving of problems of structural unemployment must thus clearly be facilitated by success in reducing 'Keynesian' unemployment (the sort that can be eliminated by a sufficient rise in the level of demand). Moreover, even if all of the unemployment had been due to structural factors, it would still be worth while trying to find the best combination of measures for minimising the rate of inflation at any given level of activity.

In short, nothing in this book is intended to argue against the desirability of policies directed at overcoming structural problems; and if appropriate macroeconomic measures are adopted, the problems of structural unemployment are likely to appear—and, indeed, to be in fact—much less formidable and more readily solved.

If inflationary mixes of macroeconomic measures have been adopted, moreover, governments become tempted to place excessive blame upon alleged structural difficulties to explain the very high levels of unemployment that have in fact been caused by their adoption of inappropriate mixes of macroeconomic measures, and by their excessive reliance on deflation, rather than an appropriate mix, for trying to hold down the rate of inflation. Indeed, such policies as these have undoubtedly had the effect of holding down real investment in many areas and industries where an insufficiency of investment has been an important reason for the structural unemployment. It is true that some types of unemployment cannot be eliminated merely by raising the level of demand; and that there may well be cases where real wage costs would also have to be reduced if unemployment were to be successfully brought down by expansionary measures. But the existence of structural unemployment is not in itself a generally valid argument against taking appropriate expansionary measures.

THE POLICY MIX AND PRICES AND INCOMES POLICY

Many people place considerable stress on the need to hold back wages (and other incomes) and prices by some form of voluntary or compulsory restraint as a means of reconciling high levels of activity with no more than a tolerable rate of inflation. Views may reasonably differ about the feasibility and desirability of such policies. The present section considers some of the ways in which the proposals made in the two preceding chapters about the appropriate mix of macroeconomic measures may interact with any attempts being made to apply some sort of prices and incomes policy.

Some proponents of prices and incomes policies may be tempted to oppose any other suggestions for ways of reconciling high levels of activity with the avoidance of excessive inflation, on the grounds that if governments (and unions and employers) believe there is some other method of solving the basic macroeconomic problem, they are less likely to agree to the degree of restraint in the setting of wages and prices that may be necessary. If we can be confident that there are forms of prices and incomes policy available that would succeed, and that they would work without imposing considerable real costs, and especially if we have doubts about the alternative measures proposed, these reservations may have some justification. But it cannot reasonably be argued that the feasibility and reliability of prices and incomes policies are great enough, and the potential costs of operating them slight enough, for us to be justified in neglecting any other potentially useful ways of reconciling high levels of activity with the control of inflation.

Moreover, the adoption of an anti-inflationary policy mix should increase the likelihood of success for any prices and incomes policy; for the chances of such policies breaking down are increased if the other policy weapons are not used in ways that will also contribute to the aim of controlling inflation whilst maintaining a high level of employment. It is a far more reasonable approach to try to use all the available instruments to achieve the desired aims of macroeconomic policy.

There is, however, a very real danger that the considerable expenditure of political and intellectual effort that is required to make a prices and incomes policy become widely accepted, and so to make it work, will divert attention and effort from the task of securing an appropriate mix of the principal macroeconomic instruments. For it is important that there should be a wide and deep public understanding of the relative effects on the price level and on the level of activity of each of the various instruments, if the most appropriate mix of macroeconomic measures is to receive public acceptance. If public attention is focused instead mainly upon trying to secure some sort of prices and incomes policy (or a 'freeze' or 'pause'), rather than on making it politically possible to achieve a mix of measures that can achieve a high level of activity without inflation, the prices and incomes policy itself is likely to break down eventually, even if it seems to be successful in its initial stages.

Indeed, there is one particular respect in which undue concentration on prices and incomes policies—especially in the crude form of a 'freeze'—may make it hard or impossible to implement the mix of macroeconomic measures that will probably be necessary in order to curb inflation whilst maintaining a high level of activity. This is the view that is sometimes taken in popular discussion that when prices and incomes are 'frozen' or held down, interest rates should also be kept low. For if this is the necessary price to be paid in order to obtain public acceptance of a 'freeze' or 'pause' it will often mean that tax rates will have to be kept higher (at any given level of activity) than would otherwise be necessary, so that cost-push inflation from that source, as well as price inflation through the direct effect of the monetary measures needed to hold down interest rates, will be consequently higher than if interest rates had been left to rise instead. If low interest rates are thought of as part of a prices and incomes policy, therefore, the chances of any prices and incomes policy succeeding are correspondingly weaker. On the other hand, it is, of course, also true that so far as the prices and incomes policy is in fact successful, the ultimate result will be lower (nominal) interest rates than if inflation had been at a higher rate. It is therefore a perfectly sensible aim to try to bring about a situation where nominal rates of interest come down naturally; but a policy of trying to hold them down will make inflation worse and thus make any form of prices and incomes policy correspondingly less likely to succeed.

Those who consider some form of prices and incomes policy essential and feasible should regard such an approach as being complementary to that adopted in this book; for without an appropriate mix of monetary and budgetary measures any prices and incomes policy is likely to fail, but with an appropriate mix the chances of success will be much greater.

Those who believe prices and incomes policies to be harmful or unworkable should emphasise the need to choose an appropriate mix, as that will reduce the risk of governments trying to implement harmful prices and incomes policies; and if they do pursue such policies, the choice of a non-inflationary mix will minimise the pressure placed on the prices and incomes policies, and therefore the damage they are likely to do.

Would the Suggested Mix Prejudice Prices and Incomes Policy?

One way of trying to enforce restraint in wage settlements is to raise the credible threat of creating more unemployment if wage rates rise too rapidly; for example, by declaring a target rate of growth for the money supply, at a rate that would imply a rise in unemployment if money wage rates rose above a certain, tolerable, rate. If unions are as concerned about the numbers unemployed as they are about the incomes of their employed members, this approach may succeed; but if they are mainly concerned with the incomes of those of their members that remain in employment, it will not.

If, however, there are ways of reducing the rate of inflation other than that of creating a high level of unemployment, the threat that excessive wage increases will lead to more unemployment will become still weaker. Even whilst keeping within a declared monetary target, it should be possible to reduce prices by tax cuts coupled with bond sales, rather than by resorting to bringing about more unemployment. It is true that, past a certain point, it may not be practicable to bring about a change of mix in the suggested direction on a scale that will offset the upward effects of the wage increases on the price level. But the knowledge that a change of mix may be available that will at least weaken the extent of the inflation resulting from a given wage rise, might weaken the opposition to wage inflation. For it will no longer be possible to argue that the inevitable result of those wage increases will be additional unemployment (at least provided that the government adheres to the money supply target that it has adopted).

On the other hand, readiness on the part of the government to vary its macroeconomic policy mix in directions that will hold down prices at any given level of activity could act as a very effective restraint on income demands. In particular, income demands are often a reaction against falling real disposable income, not only as a result of rising prices, but also as a result of rising tax rates.

If a government agrees to cut taxes as part of a bargain with unions over wage increases it may feel that it is tying its hands; and it may doubt whether this is a good bargain, especially if it feels that the unions cannot guarantee to restrain wage increases to the extent that they have undertaken. A better sort of bargain from the country's point of view would presumably be one that commits the government to raising taxes all round if money wage settlements prove subsequently to be too high. Ideally, the unions and the government would therefore agree in advance that there would be a sliding scale of tax rates (or at least income tax rates), which would vary according to the rate of increase in wage rates or earnings over the period covered by the bargain. This would also overcome the difficulty that if the bargain about income tax rates and wage increases were struck in advance each side might try to insist that the other show its hand first; for the unions would naturally prefer the government to announce its tax schedule before they give an undertaking about wage demands, whilst the government would naturally wish the unions to give their undertaking first, and then to respond by announcing the income tax schedule that it would apply.

But if the bargain reached was to the effect that a certain rate of increase in money wage rates or in earnings would lead to the application of a particular schedule of income tax rates, whilst a faster increase in pretax earnings would lead to the application of a higher schedule of income tax rates, the effect would be that the real post-tax earnings of employees would be guaranteed—yet also limited—in aggregate terms by the government, in such a way that rapid increases in pretax incomes would become pointless from the viewpoint of the wage-earner. Indeed, if this principle could be taken further it would be possible to ensure that real post-tax earnings over the period covered by the bargain. This would also slowly than they would be if money wage rates rose rapidly This would give an incentive to those who negotiate for higher wage rates to moderate their demands, in the knowledge that the real post-tax earnings of those for whom they were negotiating would actually be higher if their pretax earnings grew only at a modest rate. It would be perfectly reasonable for a government to reach such an agreement with trade unions, because the higher is the rate of inflation in a country, the less willing is a government likely to be to allow the economy to operate at or near full employment. This means that, other things equal, it will need to impose higher real tax rates if money incomes rise rapidly than it would need to do if they rose only slowly, as in the latter case the problem of inflation would be correspondingly less.

SOME POSSIBLE OBJECTIONS

There are various objections that some people may be inclined to raise to the principles for improving the macroeconomic mix suggested in the two previous chapters. Although most of these objections are strictly irrational (and one of them that is in principle reasonable is not of any practical significance) the mere fact that these views are held by some people may create political and practical obstacles to the implementation of the policies, so that the objections are 'real' in this sense. Moreover, however unsound an argument against a particular policy may be analytically, if people widely believe it to be valid, this may reduce or destroy the efficacy of the policy. Where this is so, the right remedy is clearly to remove the misconceptions from which the difficulty arises. Their potential as obstacles to the adoption of rational macroeconomic policies makes it important, therefore, to discuss them; even though to do so may run the risk of dignifying some of them with more attention than could really be justified on any other grounds.

One of the most potentially powerful obstacles of this sort is the widespread fear of inflation that may be aroused by a policy that increases what may on one definition be described, at least in some countries, as the 'budget deficit'. If a budget deficit is defined (as it often is) as the difference between government outlays and government revenue, then a shift from taxation towards borrowing would on this definition increase the budget deficit, even though it need not increase the cash deficit or the money supply. The easy equating in some people's minds of a budget deficit with an increase in the money supply depends on the implicit assumption that the increase in the deficit is not financed by extra borrowing from the non-bank public—whereas in fact the policy proposed here does involve additional borrowing from the public, in a way that may be expected to reduce the price level. But it is imperative that public discussion of any such change of mix should give the same attention to this aspect of the combined package as to the effects of the tax cuts (which, taken alone, would tend to increase the 'budget deficit', on one widely used definition).

A serious psychological obstacle to the implementation of the suggested policy is the difficulty that most people have in considering the variations of two policy-instruments at the same time. This difficulty is not confined to non-economists, politicians or journalists; indeed, very senior economic policy advisers have been known to object to the proposed package for tackling stagflation on the two mutually contradictory, or at least mutually offsetting, grounds that 'cutting taxes will be inflationary, as it will increase the deficit' and (often no more than a few minutes later) 'higher interest rates will reduce activity'. Of course, both statements taken separately are true. But as complementary parts of a combined package the two measures taken together in appropriate doses can reduce the price level without changing the level of activity; and taken in appropriately different doses can provide a non-inflationary stimulus.

A third problem is that people sometimes irrationally suppose that any change in the macroeconomic mix will have effects upon the allocation of resources or on the distribution of income in directions that they will find unwelcome. But the precise types of taxes to be cut (or subsidies increased) can be chosen in such a way as to have virtually any desired effect on the allocation of resources or on the distribution of income; and if it is thought that a rise in interest rates (which may be temporary) will reduce the level of investment or of dwelling construction, for example, the tax concessions or rise in subsidies could, if this were felt to be desirable, be concentrated upon offsetting this undesired effect. Even if the house buyer or business man had given back to him by way of subsidies the same amount as he had to pay by way of extra interest, the shift in mix would still have the desired effect of reducing inflation.

TERMINOLOGY AND MACROECONOMIC OBJECTIVES

There is a real problem arising out of verbal difficulties associated with the formulation of the main issues of macroeconomic policy. Such words as 'inflation', 'reflation', 'deflation' and 'disinflation' have not generally been used in consistent and uniformly agreed meanings, by economists or the public generally. But, broadly speaking, 'inflation' has generally been used to mean 'any situation with a rising price level'; 'reflation' to mean 'the process of raising the economy from an unduly depressed level of activity'; 'deflation' to mean 'the process of reducing the economy below full employment'; and 'disinflation' to mean 'the removal of excess demand'. But even among economists one could not reasonably claim that such usages have been consistent.

Among the general public, therefore, it is not surprising that there is confusion about such usages. Furthermore, in non-English-speaking countries confusion about the meanings of the English words is, apparently, sometimes great even among economists and policy-makers. One writer said he lost count of the number of times within a week that highly placed Germans with whom he was discussing the taking of reflationary action in the German economy confused the word 'reflation' with 'inflation'. In effect this naturally created a real verbal and psychological barrier to the acceptance of measures that would raise the general level of activity in the German economy, as it seemed to imply that such measures *must by definition* raise the price level.

Another writer (not a financial journalist) in a British newspaper accused economists of trying to create an artificial difference by speaking of 'reflation' when they really meant 'inflation'. But as the crucial question of macroeconomic policy in the mid-1970s has become this very issue of finding ways to raise the level of activity without raising the rate of inflation (or, at least, with as little upward effect on it as possible), no useful purpose can be served by using words in a way that rules out by definition the possibility that the problem might be solved. Indeed, there can be no reasonable dispute that expansion is possible, at least in some circumstances, without leading to faster inflation (most obviously when there is much spare capacity, as a revival of output can in these circumstances occur with a large simultaneous fall in unit costs); so that the need for separate words that clearly differentiate the idea of inflation from that of economic recovery should be obvious. Perhaps the term 'expansion' (rather than 'reflation') should be used to mean the raising of the real level of activity (relative to capacity), and the word 'inflation' to mean 'any rise in the general price level' (at any level or rate of change of activity, up or down).

'INFLATION' AND 'UNEMPLOYMENT' AS TARGETS

The tendency to identify or confuse the concepts of 'reflation' and 'inflation' is paralleled by a tendency to consider the objective of holding down the rate of inflation as being by definition in conflict with that of holding down the level of unemployment. Politicians often make such statements as 'we have to get down the rate of inflation before we can reduce unemployment'—thereby implicitly assuming that the two objectives require opposing policies. We have no single word to describe what is the real aim of macroeconomic policy, namely, to maintain full employment while holding down inflation to zero (or even a negative rate), or at least as low as possible. The aim of thereby minimising macroeconomic misery can be summed up in some situations as 'stopping stagflation'; and in a world economy where there is much spare capacity and high rates of inflation, this phrase—'minimising macroeconomic misery'—is about as succinct as the writer can suggest. But once one focuses only on stopping inflation, or only on reducing unemployment, one is liable to lose sight of the costs that may (or may not) be involved in terms of the other objective.

If, however, the economy in question cannot be said to be 'stagnating', but is merely suffering from something slightly less than full employment (or if it is already at full employment; or even in a state of excess demand) one requires a single term to embody the aim of maintaining or restoring full employment with no more than a minimum (if any) upward effect on the price level. No such phrase exists (so far as the writer is aware). One might like to use the phrase 'internal balance', but that has been used in the past to describe a state of 'full employment' only, whereas one wants a phrase that embodies also the aim of keeping down the rate of inflation at any given level of activity, as well as seeing that total real demand is kept at an appropriate level.

Perhaps one might use the (cumbersome) phrase 'internal balance with price stability', though this begs the question of what is meant by 'price stability', and of whether the general level of prices should be rising or falling (and at what rate) or whether it should be absolutely stable. But if one accepts that this particular target (of the rate of inflation) has to be left somewhat vague, such a phrase—'internal balance with price stability'—may serve the purpose of emphasising that the appropriate target for macroeconomic policy has these two dimensions, and thus make it harder for policy-makers or those discussing policy to focus exclusively or disproportionately on one of them.

THE NATIONAL DEBT AND THE POLICY MIX

If there were a stable price level and no expectation of inflation, there would be some level of government borrowing from the non-bank public that would be ideal from the viewpoint of the community as a whole at full employment, given the proportion of government spending to total output that was thought desirable. The question to be considered here is whether in an economy suffering from stagflation the aim of holding down the rate of inflation should influence the relative importance to be attached to tax-financing and bond-financing respectively. We will assume that the share of government spending to total output is to be kept at the same level as would prevail in the absence of inflation.

As the reduction of inflation is of some social benefit, clearly some degree of (gross) social cost will be worth incurring in order to bring it about, even if the economy would in any case be operated at full employment. If a shift towards bond-financing can do something to reduce the price level or the rate of inflation over some period, therefore, it will be worth making such a shift—up to the point at which any additional social costs of the shift of mix will just equal the additional social benefit that results from reducing the rate of inflation at the given (full employment) level of activity.

We have seen that a shift towards more bond-financing and away from tax-financing is likely to reduce the rate of inflation, provided that the taxes reduced were having some degree of cost-push effect (at any given level of activity), and as any accompanying rise in interest rates may well reduce, and will not increase, the rate of inflation. For we have seen that a large sale of bonds—with at least temporarily higher nominal interest rates and reduction in the money supply—will have at least some once-and-for-all downward effect on the price level, at any given level of activity. For one or both of these reasons a shift from tax-financing towards bond-financing will have some effect in the direction of reducing the rate of inflation.

Let us now consider the implications of using a rise in the level of the national debt for the purpose of holding down the upward pressure on the price level, at a given level of activity. The immediate social benefits will include whatever advantages are believed to result from a diminution of the upward pressure on the price level, and also from the better use of resources that will follow if this shift makes possible a lower level of taxation. Whatever costs a larger national debt may impose on posterity—and there is room for a good deal of divergence of views about whether these are real costs and about how important they will be—it must be true that the benefits to be derived from checking the upward pressure on the price level in the near future will bring benefits that will justify a higher level of borrowing from the public than would otherwise have been warranted. This will be true (to some extent) whatever weight one gives to the interests of posterity and whatever one's views about the ability of future generations to bear any extra costs that this may impose on them.

But we have to consider also the benefits that posterity will derive from a more successful achievement by the present generation of its macroeconomic objectives. Even within the present assumption that we merely reduce the upward pressure on the price level each time some bonds are sold, but do not consequently decide to operate the economy at a higher level of activity, there should be some potential gains for posterity (as well as to ourselves). For the reduction in the rate of inflation (over the relevant period) may be expected also to reduce inflation in future, so far as that will depend on expectations about inflation, and so far as these expectations in turn depend upon the level of prices that has been experienced in the past. If the mix of measures that we choose helps in this way to reduce inflation in future, that may therefore be a benefit in itself. It may also mean that future governments will consequently be less inclined to permit a high level of unemployment to persist, with the aim of thereby checking inflation. For these reasons, if a rise in the level of bond-financing does no more than restrain the upward pressure on prices at a given level of activity in the present, that may in itself bring some benefit to posterity.

We must now add, however, the major benefit to posterity that can be expected to result from our adoption of a mix of macroeconomic measures that helps to restrain the level of prices in the present and near future. This is the additional output, including the higher level of investment, that will be possible if the less inflationary mix leads governments to operate the economy at nearer to full employment than they would otherwise have chosen.

For posterity will reap some of the fruits of the larger stock of capital that is to be expected as a result. If we are in a situation of stagflation, therefore, the case for a shift of mix towards bond-financing is stronger, not only from the point of view of this generation, but also from the viewpoint of future generations.

It should also be borne in mind that this analysis began with the assumption that the level of government borrowing is already at the level which would be ideal in the absence of the need to restrain inflation. If the actual level of government borrowing is less than this, however, the implication is that a shift in the direction of a higher level of government borrowing (in relation to total output) will bring other social benefits, in addition to contributing towards reducing inflation. In any actual situation, therefore, the government ought to consider what level of the national debt would be ideal from other points of view, and then to adjust the level of its financing in the direction of more borrowing and less taxation, to the extent that it wishes to make use of this sort of change of mix with the aim of reducing inflation.

It is especially important to reconsider such matters at the present time, as the very high rates of inflation in recent years have been greatly reducing the real value of the accumulated national debt and of the interest payments on it. This is usually acceptable to governments and their advisers, though it represents a form of repudiation of the debt without any due process of law, and without any avenue of redress for bond-holders.

Moreover—at least as important for our present purposes—this eating away of the real value of the securities owned by the public, and of the interest on them, may well be playing an important role in perpetuating and worsening stagflation. For as people add to their accumulated savings each year they want to purchase a certain flow of appropriate financial assets. If private industry is unable or unwilling to provide such securities on a sufficient scale it is especially important that the government should provide a sufficient supply of them. As the role of the government sector in most countries has substantially increased in recent decades, many functions that might in the past have been performed by private industry, and financed by borrowing, have been taken over by governments; and as the latter may try to finance some of these functions by raising taxes or charges (or by the creation of money) instead of by selling securities to the public, it is likely that unless due care is taken by governments to maintain an adequate supply of financial assets in forms suited to the needs of lenders, the total supply of such financial assets on attractive terms will not be adequate. If this happens, savers will seek to hold their savings in more attractive forms such as real estate, antiques and so on. As the stock of real assets is fixed at any given point in time, and at any given level of activity, the effect of this will be to raise the price level of real assets. Furthermore, so far as the particular goods chosen as real assets in which to accumulate savings are not limited in supply, more of them may be produced and the pattern of production will to that extent be distorted away from the pattern that would have been chosen if an adequate supply of securities on appropriate terms had been available to meet the requirements of savers. Private borrowers have an incentive to meet such demands for appropriate securities, up to the level of their borrowing requirements. But as governments have a wider range of alternative forms of financing open to them, including taxation, they may not issue sufficient by way of financial assets to prevent savers from forcing up the prices of the existing stock of real assets and increasing the production of the types of goods that they want for this purpose above the level that would be ideal on more fundamental criteria.

This is likely to be especially true in periods of rapid inflation. For the real value of the national debt held by the public is likely to be declining in relation to total incomes or output, so that savers find themselves increasingly obliged to hold additions to their savings in other forms—which means in some sort of real assets. Treasury officials may become understandably appalled at the high ratio of interest payments on the national debt in relation to total budget outlays; for in a period when rapid inflation is expected high nominal rates of interest have to be offered in order to sell bonds at all. Yet if the reaction of the government is to try to sell bonds to a lower total value (in relation to national income, or to people's needs for these as their incomes rise), the resulting reduction in nominal interest rates will further stimulate inflation by increasing the relative attractiveness of goods and consequently worsening the allocation of resources.

Furthermore, as we have seen in Chapter 4, the adoption of an inappropriate policy mix—one that causes an unnecessarily large increase in the price level in the process of bringing about an expansion—also tends to be rendered less effective (and may even, eventually, be totally ineffective) as a result of two repercussions. The first of these is the tendency for money wage rates to rise in the wake of rapid price increases (at any given level of activity) by more than they would if prices were rising more slowly or not at all; and the second is the tendency for people to try to rebuild their real balances of cash and other liquid assets, by saving more out of a given income than they would otherwise do, when their accumulated liquid assets have become lower (in real terms) than they would normally wish to hold, as a result of rising prices. (As the extent of this effect is very hard to predict, it adds considerably to the problems of maintaining full employment.)

This means that if a government adopts an inflationary policy mix it is likely to be less successful in maintaining a high level of activity, even if it is making as much effort to do so as it would have done in the absence of any concern about the rate of inflation. If, therefore, the sale of bonds reduces the extent of a rise in the price level, it may also make a government's efforts to maintain full employment more successful. If so, this will constitute a further consequential potential benefit accruing to both the present and future generations as a result of the adoption of a less inflationary policy mix; and so an additional social benefit to set against any social cost that may be felt likely to result from a rise in the national debt. As output and revenue revived, fewer bonds would need to be sold.

It would clearly be absurd to argue that a shift of mix towards bond-financing is undesirable simply on the grounds that there is presumably some upper limit to the extent to which the national debt ought to be increased. For one would have to establish that the debt or the interest on it was already (on some reasonable criterion) so great that any social gain from reducing the rate of inflation, as a result of a shift to bond-financing, would not be worth achieving, even if it made possible the operation of the economy at a higher level of activity, as well as a consequently higher output of desirable goods and services at any given level of activity. In fact, however, if the shift to bond-financing does result in an increase in the available output of goods and services, it is highly unlikely that posterity will suffer. For one of the best things we can do for posterity is to stop stagflation. If a shift to bond-financing is one element in the mix required to make this possible, posterity is unlikely to thank us for being so concerned about the level of the national debt that we fail to stop stagflation. But if we are really overcome by this quaint, old-fashioned concern about the possible costs to posterity of a rise in the national debt, we still have the alternative of restraining the rate of increase in government spending (which we have so far in our discussion of the national debt been taking as given) and also taxation as a proportion of total output, so long as there are any cost-push taxes to be reduced or any cost-reducing subsidies that can be paid. We may at first thereby forego some government spending on goods and services that we would have liked to undertake. But as the object of the change of mix will be to make possible a higher level of total output, it is unlikely that we will for long have to do without any really desirable forms of government spending. The choice between bond sales and cuts in government spending (as alternative ways of making possible a reduction in taxation) ought therefore to be taken on the criterion of the best allocation of resources. If the level of government spending is such that there are no directions in which it is of social benefit to reduce it (at least as a proportion of total output), it is highly unlikely that the alternative of a rise in debt owed to the public will inflict net social costs on the community (present and future) comparable to those that will result from permitting stagflation to continue unchecked.

There are, then, considerable social benefits for posterity to derive from the adoption of a policy mix that will stop stagflation. These benefits would have to be set against any costs that we feel we are imposing on posterity if a rise in the national debt is one element in the policy mix.

In practice, however, governments are highly unlikely to be particularly concerned with such remote issues as the welfare of posterity; and the difficulty of making any reasonably reliable predictions about the strength of these considerations makes it virtually impossible to do so. Indeed, most governments have a time-horizon that is for most purposes more or less limited to the next election. If they could be sure that a given change of mix would enable them to overcome stagflation before the election, they would be highly unlikely to refrain from adopting it out of concern for future generations. But this very fact may sometimes lead conscientious economic advisers to stress, and even to overstress, the possible costs to future generations of a large rise in the national debt. In principle this conscientious approach is admirable, and it might be hoped that the putting of this point of view by advisers would be a useful corrective to what one might expect to be the natural predisposition of politicians to take too short a view.

But, in the present context, it is important to ask that in taking decisions on such matters policy-makers and their advisers should make every effort to attach appropriate weights to *all* the potential costs and benefits; and that this should include the social benefits to both the present and future generations of overcoming inflation—and especially of stopping stagflation. A shift towards a greater degree of bond-financing may constitute the crucial contribution towards achieving that aim.

THE NATIONAL DEBT AND THE LEVEL OF CONSUMPTION

The long-run effects of the issue of bonds to the public include any effects there may be on consumption (at any level of income) that may be caused by the rise in their financial wealth as a result of the bond issues. In the short run a government can probably ignore this, but a progressive rise in the level of the national debt held by the non-bank public may have effects that will require to be taken into account in the framing of macroeconomic policy decisions.

If we compare the effects of a given level of government spending financed by an issue of bonds to the public with the same level of government spending financed by taxation (assuming initially, for simplicity, that the same level of tax receipts as of bond sales is required to hold down private demand to the required extent), the bond-financing alternative presumably leaves the public with larger holdings of financial wealth than they would have held if taxes had been levied instead (though the market price of each bond will probably be lower). The bond-financing alternative may thus be expected to lead to a higher level of consumption in future than if the taxes had been levied instead; in order to prevent private demand from rising to above the desired level at some future time, therefore, the extent of bond sales may have to be correspondingly greater; or taxes may have to be levied, or government spending reduced in future, in order to prevent a rise in spending as a result of the rise in financial wealth of the public.

On the other hand, some people have suggested that when there is a rise in the national debt, and in the nominal interest payable on it, people may take into account the extra taxation that they may expect to be levied on them in order to finance the consequently higher level of debt-servicing, and may reduce their spending accordingly. This is probably no more than a interesting fiction in the minds of some imaginative economists; but if anyone does react in this way his consumption will be lower (for any given level of bonds held by him).

One effect of the issue of bonds by the government will presumably be to reduce the scale of bond issues by companies. The financial wealth of individuals may to that extent be no higher than if government bond sales had been on a smaller scale. It is true that if the private sector issues fewer bonds, the liabilities that members of the public owe to one another are lower, and in principle any effects this may have on the consumption of borrowers and of lenders should offset one another—and probably do so when one individual is lending to another. But it is by no means certain that members of the public react in their capacity as shareholders to the knowledge that their company has issued more fixed-interest securities by reducing their consumption to the same extent (if they do so at all) as they would increase their consumption as a result of holding some of these securities. If the individual members of the public hold a given total of financial assets, therefore, the level of their consumption out of a given income is likely to be much the same, whether securities issued by companies represent a larger or a smaller proportion of the total (compared with the proportion represented by government bonds). Moreover, there is no reason to expect the level of real investment by companies to be lower in the case where they issue relatively large amounts of securities to the public; indeed, the resources made available to the private sector by these borrowings (as a result of the government having borrowed correspondingly less) will presumably enable private investment to be at much the same level as it would have been if the alternative of high taxation had been chosen as the means of holding down the resources available to companies.

It is possible that private companies may reduce the level of their investment as a result of a large rise in the national debt, in the belief that it indicates some sort of government irresponsibility. If so, this factor would tend to offset the upward effects on demand that may result from the greater financial wealth of the public under the bond-financing alternative.

In short, there may or may not be long-run repercussions (in either direction) on the level of private spending as a result of a rise in the public's holdings of government bonds. But, so far as there are such effects, the level of borrowing by the government required to have a given effect on private demand will be correspondingly greater or less. The required difference between the government's receipts and outlays, and therefore the net change required in the money supply, will therefore depend partly on these direct considerations; and it may well also be different in the long run from that which will be required in the short run.

Minimising any Rise in the 'Debt Burden' if Inflation is Checked

If a government sells a large amount of bonds at a very high nominal rate of interest, and then (partly as a result of this) successfully checks inflation, it will certainly leave some lucky bond-holders with an asset bearing a very high real rate of return.

The size of the 'burden' imposed by this on taxpayers in the future is not likely to be a large one, if one starts from a point at which the real post-tax return to lenders has been low or negative: it would have to rise to a very high positive figure before a government could justifiably see this as a real obstacle to adopting the sort of macroeconomic mix suggested above.

But a government would do well to take steps to minimise this burden in future if it can do so without sacrificing the immediate benefits of adopting the proposed anti-inflationary mix.

At one extreme, the policy of the government subsequently writing down unilaterally the nominal value of interest and principal of these bonds might be envisaged. It might be argued that people had bought them at very high nominal rates of interest only because the market at that time expected a high rate of inflation; and that when inflation has been greatly reduced it is therefore not unreasonable to reduce the nominal rate of return on them. But it would be thoroughly reprehensible for governments to default unliterally (even partially in this way) on their legal obligations. It would be greatly preferable that when the bonds were issued it should be stipulated that if inflation were reduced below a certain rate (as measured by some widely accepted official index) the nominal return on the bonds should be reduced to a lower level.

This would, however, be an untidy second best to issuing bonds whose interest and principal are, from the outset, linked to an official price index. But if governments are reluctant to introduce index-linked securities on a large scale (which they seem to be) it would be absurd to refrain from a mix of macroeconomic policy measures that gives a good hope of checking inflation, simply on account of the fear that it might succeed—and that that would inflict on posterity a real tax burden larger than the existing government would wish. It would thus be best, from this and other points of view, to face up to the (real or imagined) difficulties of introducing index-linked bonds, especially if governments do see the future real-tax burden of a large national debt (at high nominal rates) as a genuine obstacle to adopting a policy mix involving large bond sales, coupled with lower taxes. The probability is, however, that where governments or their advisers express objections of this sort, this is primarily an excuse for not facing up to the problems of issuing sufficiently attractive (or, at least, honest) bonds. For managers of the national debt have now experienced many years in which continuous inflation and low real interest rates have in effect unilaterally written down a large part of the debt owed by governments to the public; and so, incidentally, given governments a strong interest in allowing inflation to continue.

WHY WON'T GOVERNMENTS REDUCE TAXES?

A prescription for generally lower tax rates should be politically popular: it is therefore somewhat surprising that governments have so widely failed to apply it in the cost-push inflationary world of the recent past. But one reason has probably been the (politically) comparatively painless tax increases that have resulted from inflation itself when tax scales have been progressive. If increases in effective tax rates had always had to be announced as such they would have been less likely to occur. The (downward) indexation of income-tax scales to the rate of inflation (such as has been introduced in a few countries) might therefore well contribute towards the establishment of a more appropriate mix of monetary and budgetary measures.

A still more potent reason may well be that many treasury and central bank officials seem to feel it to be among their prime responsibilities to keep down 'the burden of the national debt' (even if it is already being rapidly reduced by high rates of inflation) and to keep up tax revenue—almost as objectives in their own right, and without taking into account all the various social costs and benefits of the sort of mix of measures to which these biases give rise. This duty (as many advisers see it) may therefore very well be in dangerous conflict with the social interests of the community, if the aim of reducing inflation and simultaneously reducing unemployment can best be achieved by cutting taxes and selling bonds.

Problems of Timing

A government might accept in principle the view that a stimulus brought about by a tax cut (or a cost-reducing subsidy) coupled with bond sales causes a non-inflationary expansion, yet be unwilling to adopt the package of measures because it feared that the downward effects on the price level resulting from either or both of these measures might take some time, whilst the political odium of any temporary rise there might be in nominal interest rates would be immediate, and the political benefit of the non-inflationary recovery might be too long delayed. It is therefore worth discussing ways in which any time-lags could be minimised.

The requirement is that the funds borrowed by the government should be immediately channelled into keeping down costs and prices. If they were channelled directly into reductions in taxes, or increases in subsidies, on wage payments, those important costs of businesses would be held down and employment therefore stimulated; whilst prices, so far as they depended on costs, would also be kept down. If there were about to be a wage increase—as a result of collective bargaining or arbitration—the payment of part or all of the wage rise by the government (out of funds borrowed for the purpose) would enable business costs to remain at their former level, and yet to give a stimulus to activity as a result of the rise in the disposable incomes of wage-earners.

If the government's immediate concern is to reduce prices directly, rather than money wage rates, the quickest way to do this would be to pay direct subsidies on products of widespread consumption, on condition that their prices were reduced accordingly.

So far as prices and wage costs in the community were held down by these measures, the demand for money (at a given level of activity) would also be held down. If the sale of bonds were sufficient to cover this, and to permit an expansion of the real money supply only sufficient to make possible a rise in activity without a rise in the price level, an expansion with price stability would be possible. Indeed, some degree of expansion with both price stability and stability of interest rates would be possible. For the fall in the price level will reduce the demand for money, and if bond sales are just sufficient to leave the money supply unchanged, the real level of activity could rise sufficiently to absorb the money so released without any rise in interest rates. The bigger the cuts in cost-push taxes coupled with bond sales that a government undertakes, the bigger the rise in the real level of activity it can have (with a given money supply) without a rise in the price level; and the fall in the rate of inflation may reduce interest rates.

Could Expansionary Monetary Measures Increase Interest Rates?

Even assuming that expenditure reacts in the normal way to a change in interest rates brought about by monetary policy—that is, by rising when interest rates are reduced—it is possible that the final situation after the monetary expansion would be one in which interest rates were actually higher. This would happen if the stimulus to investment (and perhaps also to consumption) were so great that the consequent increase in the demand for money exceeded the injection of money into the economy through the original monetary measure of expansion. But, if this were true, the rise in interest rates brought about by the same real stimulus through budgetary measures would be even greater, as in that case there would have been no rise in the money supply to meet some of the extra demand for money as activity rose. For this reason, the principles on which the choice should be made between monetary and budgetary measures would thus still be the same as we have outlined above. For it would be true in this case also that interest rates would rise by more under the budgetary stimulus than they would with the equivalent monetary stimulus. It would also be true in this case that expansionary monetary measures would stimulate activity.

In this respect there would therefore be an important contrast with the case discussed in the previous chapter—where the possibility was considered that a reduction in interest rates through monetary measures might actually reduce total demand. Both of these cases can be depicted as a 'perversely sloping' IS schedule—that is, one in which higher levels of activity are associated with higher interest rates when planned saving is in equilibrium with planned investment. But, as we have seen in the text, the policy implications of the two cases are radically different. For if the reason for the perverse slope is that a cut in interest rates actually reduces total demand, monetary policy of the orthodox sort is obviously worse than useless for stimulating activity. But if the reason is merely that any form of stimulation raises the demand for money especially sharply, monetary policy can still stimulate activity, but will raise interest rates in the process (though not as much as will an equivalent budgetary stimulus).

What if a Tax Cut Actually Reduced Prices?

The case for cutting cost-push taxes argued above depended on the proposition that the stimulus to demand given by such a measure would have less upward effect on the price level or the rate of inflation than an otherwise equivalent stimulus given by monetary means, or by a rise in government spending. It was not argued that the stimulus provided by a tax cut would have no upward effect at all on the price level.

It is, however, possible that if the taxes cut were ones that were having very great upward effects on the price level or on wage rates there might even be an actual downward effect on the price level as a result of tax cuts. We have now to ask what would be the implications for policy if that were so.

The principal implication would be that tax cuts would then become an ideal way of stopping stagflation, as they would give a stimulus to employment whilst actually reducing the price level below what it would have been without the cuts in tax rates. In this sense there would thus be no need for supporting action from monetary measures or government spending. But it would also mean that if the taxes were cut, the price level could be held constant even with some appreciable expansion of the level of activity and of the money supply, so that some or all of the tax cuts could be financed by the creation of money without this raising the price level.

But no government could be sure whether the taxes it was cutting were so cost-push for it to safely reduce them without taking contractionary monetary measures to offset any net upward effect the measure might have on the price level—if taxes were cut without offsetting monetary measures. One could, however, suggest that if the taxes that are being reduced are thought to be very cost-push a cut in them should be the main measure adopted, and a process of trial and error should then determine whether the supporting monetary policy needed to be neutral or contractionary—or conceivably even expansionary. At least one could still say with confidence that a cut in cost-push tax rates would be the one essential element in a policy to stop stagflation—whatever the supplementary monetary policy might turn out to be.

What if Interest Rates are More Cost-push than Taxes?

It has been argued above (in Chapter 3) that the various ways in which high tax rates are cost-push inflationary must, on any reasonable expectation, exceed any net cost-push effect that there might be from high interest rates (and, indeed, that high interest rates can be expected on balance to hold down the price level or the rate of inflation at a given level of activity).

But, for completeness, something should be said about what policy should be adopted if a government were convinced that the reverse were true. One might imagine a situation where all cost-push taxes had been eliminated, and where the machinery that would have to be established to implement the payment of anti-cost-push subsidies was felt likely to involve a waste of resources that would make it harder to control inflation; so that the further payment of anti-cost-push subsidies was thought more likely to put upward pressure on the price level than would an expansionary monetary policy—though the farfetched nature of these assumptions underlines the purely hypothetical nature of the problem.

If this situation ever existed, naturally the appropriate prescription in a stagflationary closed economy would be to ease monetary policy and tighten budgetary policy. It should be noted, however, that there would still be a mix of measures that would be available to overcome inflation without creating unemployment; if, therefore, one wishes to take the view that high interest rates are actually cost-push inflationary, one cannot proceed from that view to deny the existence of an appropriate policy mix to overcome unemployment without causing inflation. The principle involved is still the same, though the precise mix that should be chosen will be different.

It is therefore worth pointing out that a government that fails to cut taxes and sell bonds so long as it is faced by stagflation is implicitly taking the view that high interest rates are more cost-push than high tax rates. In the light of the arguments (summarised in Chapter 3) that can be marshalled for the view that high taxes raise the price level by more than high interest rates, governments should be expected to justify publicly the grounds on which they are attempting to apply the policy mix that would follow from denying that conclusion.

What if Taxes are Very Cost-push and High Interest Rates Stimulate Demand?

We have discussed above the possibility that tax rates may be so cost-push that a reduction in them will actually tend to hold down the price level, despite the stimulus that this would give to demand. We have also discussed the possibility that a rise in real post-tax interest rates could actually stimulate activity, especially if real returns to the lender have been negative, and savers have therefore been inclined to reduce their consumption, in an attempt to rebuild their financial assets towards a level where they will yield an adequate income for retirement (or against the possibility of their becoming unemployed) (see Chapter 4, page 75). Both these cases may appear to be unusual or unlikely, though neither is inconceivable. (But the present writer would regard them as far less hypothetical than the case considered in the immediately preceding section where high interest rates were assumed to be more cost-push inflationary than high tax rates.)

It is therefore worth asking what would be the implications for the policy mix if a country found itself in a situation where a rise in real interest rates would stimulate activity, and where, at the same time, a cut in tax rates (taken alone) would reduce the price level. If an economy with those characteristics was facing stagflation, and if it pursued the policy mix proposed in earlier chapters, it would cut tax rates and sell bonds. The tax cut would place downward pressure on the price level and stimulate activity; the tighter monetary policy would also tend to hold down prices and stimulate activity. Both measures would therefore tend to correct stagflation in both its aspects. It would not, therefore, greatly matter which of them had a comparative advantage or disadvantage in achieving which macroeconomic objective. The use of the normal proposed policy mix to correct stagflation would thus be appropriate. If, however, it was possible to say that a tax cut would do more than a rise in interest rates to hold down the price level (for a given stimulus to activity), the principle should be to go on cutting taxes until inflation was stopped, and to go on raising interest rates until full employment was reached. If, however, a tight monetary policy was relatively more effective in holding down the price level, such a policy should be pursued until inflation was stopped, and taxes cut until full employment was established—just as in the normal situation underlying the basic proposals in this book. The wrong mix would thus be doubly disastrous in this case.

Summary of Unusual Cases

Let us summarise the policy prescriptions applicable to the unusual or unlikely cases that have just been considered; and see how the application of the basic policy prescription for tackling stagflation would perform in an economy that turned out to have the characteristics of these special cases.

The only situation in which the basic policy prescription would not work would be in an economy where high interest rates were more cost-push than high taxes having the same effect on activity. But this cannot be rated a real possibility (for reasons argued in Chapter 3). Moreover, in a world where there is an unprecedented degree of stagflation, at the same time as real post-tax interest rates are low or even negative (again, to an extent unprecedented over any substantial period in the past), and with tax rates high in relation to total output, it is a reasonable presumption that these characteristics are connected with the existence of stagflation; in other words, that the stagflation is associated with a level of real interest rates that is too low and a level of tax rates that is too high. The case of interest rates being cost-push (to a greater extent than tax rates having the same effect on activity) is therefore likely to be no more than a hypothetical curiosity.

But the other cases are worthy of attention. As we have seen, a rise in real interest rates (especially from a low or negative level) may well stimulate activity. But, if so, the prescription of a tight monetary policy combined with tax cuts will work in the direction of overcoming stagflation; indeed, tight monetary policy alone would succeed in doing so. If it should happen that taxes were so cost-push that a reduction in tax rates reduced the price level as well as stimulating activity, tax cuts alone would overcome stagflation. If both these situations were present simultaneously, the policy prescription of tight money and tax cuts would certainly work; the only qualification being that if one knew for certain that tax cuts did more to reduce the price level (for a given real stimulus) than would a given rise in real interest rates one would continue cutting tax rates till inflation was stopped, and raising interest rates until full employment was restored; whereas in the more orthodox situation one would raise interest rates until inflation was stopped and cut tax rates until full employment was restored.

In short, in any reasonably likely situation the basic prescription to overcome stagflation should work. But in all the cases it will be safe to cut cost-push tax rates, the only reservation being about how far this should be backed up by a tighter monetary policy (or whether in some circumstances an easier monetary policy might just possibly be justified).

APPRAISING A MIX TO STOP STAGFLATION

In any package that can stop stagflation (that is, simultaneously reduce both inflation and unemployment) each individual element must (in some way) seem to be 'wrong', in the sense that each constituent measure must be open to criticism for failing to promote one object or the other. Similarly, any change in a macroeconomic weapon could seem to be justified on the grounds that it would help to achieve either lower unemployment or lower inflation. Appraisals based on such simple criteria are therefore obviously worthless. But the tendency of some people to oppose policy measures with such simplistic arguments as: 'a rise in interest rates will reduce investment'; or 'a cut in taxes will be inflationary', constitutes a major obstacle to the implementation of an appropriate mix of measures.

The grounds on which a package should be judged, therefore, are whether each particular instrument is set in the direction that will make a contribution to promoting that macroeconomic objective in which the particular instrument has a relative advantage; and whether the *combined effects* of the instruments promote *both* policy objectives.

If one considers the main instruments one by one, however, it should not be too difficult to achieve public understanding of the essential point that a tax cut will have a smaller upward effect on the price level (or a greater downward effect on it) for any given upward effect on activity than will either an expansionary monetary measure or a rise in government spending. This means that taxes should be cut until activity revives to the desired level; and that monetary policy should be tightened (by selling appropriate types of government bonds) sufficiently to offset any undesirable upward effects of the tax cuts on the money supply and the price level; for if monetary policy is tightened it is thus being directed towards affecting the policy objective (restraining the rate of inflation at a given level of activity) upon which it is relatively more effective.

In assessing the value of any critic's appraisal of a given package, therefore, one should discount his views strongly if he is criticising a monetary measure simply on the grounds that it will have a downward effect on the level of activity—or a tax reduction simply for being likely to increase the rate of inflation; for if he is doing so he has failed to grasp the essential point that the relevant criterion is the question of where their respective comparative advantages lie. Not merely have we to become accustomed to juggling at least two balls at once, we must know in which direction to throw each of them.

CONCLUSION

The discussion in this chapter of the various problems, complications and possible objections has not revealed any fundamental reason why the adoption of less inflationary types of mix should not help to keep down the rate of inflation. It has, however, drawn attention to various political and psychological problems that stand in the way of the adoption of less inflationary combinations of measures than those that have often been adopted. But as a government that moves towards a more appropriate mix will have greater success in solving the current difficult macroeconomic problems, and will be able to operate the economy at a higher level of real output, it could expect the adoption of such policies to benefit it electorally. The most serious difficulties are, in practice, likely to be the change that will need to take place in the way that people—policy-makers, journalists, economists and the public generally—think about the formulation of macroeconomic policy. The essence of this required change is the need to give as much attention to the effect of the mix of measures as to the overall effect on demand.

6 The Policy Mix in the Open Economy

In the preceding chapters we have considered the principles on which decisions should be made about the best policy mix to minimise inflation whilst maintaining a high level of activity, within the context of a closed economy. This economy may be thought of as the world as a whole, or as a first approximation to the relevant prescription for an individual country, especially a large one. But we have now to ask how the analysis has to be modified to take into account the qualifications and complications that arise when the country whose policy decisions we are considering has transactions with countries in the outside world, the governments of which it cannot control and which it will usually not be able to influence to any appreciable extent. A very large country may reasonably feel it appropriate to assume that its own actions influence the actions of other governments to some extent, and that its actions have an appreciable effect on economic events in the outside world; and also that these outside actions and events then react back on itself. The greater the extent to which it needs to take account of such repercussions as these, the closer will its position be to that of a closed economy; and the less need will there be to qualify the analysis of the preceding chapters. But most countries (probably all countries apart from the USA, and in some contexts West Germany and Japan) have to be regarded as 'small' in the sense that their policy decisions will not normally have an appreciable effect on the rest of the world; or not to such an extent that any repercussions will then react back on them in a manner that normally needs to be taken into account in forming their policies. It is the policies of 'small' countries in this sense that are being discussed in this chapter.[1]

We are considering these issues in a world where a high degree of exchange rate flexibility, in one form or another, has become the norm, in contrast to the position up to the early 1970s, when exchange rates were normally kept fixed, and then altered only infrequently but by large amounts. Nowadays smaller and more frequent alterations in exchange rates have become the general practice, though the form and extent of this exchange rate flexibility has varied greatly from country to country. We have therefore to consider whether we should use the exchange rate as an additional macroeconomic instrument, and if so how we should use it.

THE DEFICIENCIES OF DEVALUATIONS

Various doubts have been expressed about the efficacy of devaluation under contemporary conditions for its normally accepted purposes.

The first doubt is associated with the time-lag before a devaluation begins to have its expected effects in stimulating exports or reducing imports. For countries exporting manufactured goods, these doubts may arise from uncertainties about whether exporters will fix their prices at the level that is most likely to increase foreign exchange receipts, at least in the immediate aftermath of a devaluation. This may be because they are thought likely (perhaps from inertia or out of habit) to continue to charge much the same prices in terms of their own currencies for some time after devaluation (rather than raising them), and so to charge very much lower prices in terms of foreign currencies, especially if they have normally quoted prices in terms of their own currencies. If they do this, the volume of their sales may well rise little, if at all, and certainly not fully in proportion to the cut in their prices (in terms of foreign exchange), especially in the fairly short run. When devaluations were rather rare, and for countries such as Britain, whose exporters were most likely to quote their prices in their own currencies, this risk was especially great. But since exchange rates have become more flexible, there is some evidence that exporters are more likely to quote their prices in terms of external currencies, or at least to revise their quotations more frequently, so that this risk is presumably less than it used to be. The fact remains, however, that the volume of sales may take some time to respond to a change in the price quoted. It is also possible that exporters may delay a revision of their price quotations under flexible exchange rates, in order to see whether or not a depreciation will prove to be lasting.

On the other hand, it is sometimes said that exporters (again, some British exporters have been mentioned) may go to the other extreme and take out the whole of the potential gain from a devaluation by raising the prices they quote in terms of their own currency by virtually the full amount of any devaluation, thus maximising their profits per unit sold, but denying themselves the opportunity to increase their share in overseas markets by quoting lower prices (in terms of foreign exchange). Perhaps uncertainty about the length of time that a depreciation of their currencies will endure may make them reluctant to commit themselves to building up the sales and servicing facilities needed to supply a considerably larger proportion of the overseas market; or perhaps they may feel that the effort required to do so is not worth while. They may therefore prefer to accept the immediate windfall gain (in the shape of higher profit per unit exported) provided by the depreciation, rather than quote lower prices (in foreign currencies) in the hope that the volume of their sales will eventually rise sufficiently to justify that decision. Although this increases the profits of the exporters, it does nothing to increase the foreign exchange receipts of the devaluing country.[2]

Countries that export mainly primary products are not faced by quite the same sort of problems. For they are generally 'price-takers' rather than 'price-makers'—so that the prices they receive for their exports are generally fixed in world markets by forces of supply and demand outside their control. Furthermore, the supply of those products that they can put on world markets can seldom be greatly changed in the short run; so that on the export side they too may not be able to expect much rise in their receipts in terms of foreign exchange after a devaluation, at least in the reasonably short period, and perhaps even for a period of some years, while they are in the process of increasing their output of exportable commodities. This doubt about the usefulness of devaluation for increasing the exports of such countries is, of course, nothing new; but it has become of special significance of late in view of the current doubts (to be outlined below) about whether devaluation will have the expected effects on trade and output, even in the longer run.

On the import side, such a country may find that overseas supplies cannot readily be dispensed with in the short run; and for countries that are far from their main suppliers, the 'pipeline' of orders is especially long, so that even if they decide to import less after a devaluation, it may take some time before the effects show up in the volume of imports actually reaching them. It may, in any event, take some time for domestic producers to adjust their pattern of production to meeting the requirements of the domestic market after a devaluation, especially if the goods imported consist predominantly of specialised types of components, materials and capital goods required mainly by domestic industry, rather than predominantly finished products competing with the sort of goods the domestic industries are accustomed to producing.

For a country whose exports are mainly primary products, the prices of which vary in world markets readily in response to supply and demand, one might expect a devaluation to affect very speedily the internal prices of the products that are exported. Sometimes home-price schemes and similar arrangements may make this link less close. But one might certainly argue that the prices of the principal exports of such a country in terms of domestic currency are likely to rise more promptly and more nearly in proportion to a devaluation than are those of a country whose principal exports are manufactured goods, the prices of which are altered irregularly and often on the basis of cost-plus factors.

But this difference in the pattern of exports—between primary-exporting countries, on the one hand, and countries exporting manufactures on the other—also means that there is not likely to be an actual fall in the foreign exchange receipts of a primary-exporting country after a devaluation, whereas (as we have seen) there may well be a fall in the receipts of a country exporting manufactures if its exporters are dilatory about raising their quoted prices (in terms of domestic currency) after a devaluation.

Alongside the doubts about the efficacy of devaluation for improving the current account in the short run, there have in recent years been increasing doubts about its usefulness in the long run. It is often said that, just as 'money illusion' has been breaking down within countries as a result of the long experience of inflation, 'exchange rate illusion' has also been breaking down, in the sense that prices and money incomes within a devaluing country are nowadays adjusted upwards much more quickly than they used to be. It is true that if a government maintains a tight enough control over the setting of its budgetary and monetary policy this could not happen; but this merely means that the problem will then take the form of the need to accept a higher level of unemployment or of lost potential output in order to achieve a given degree of price restraint or wage restraint after a devaluation; so that the basic macroeconomic problem—which is, essentially, stagflation in some form—is intensified in one way or another. If it is true that the improvement in the balance of payments has to be brought about through creating more unemployment, it would have been preferable to adopt that means in the first place, without also having to accept the rise in the price level associated with a devaluation.

The speed with which the price rise resulting from devaluation may nowadays lead to increases in money wage rates and in other incomes and prices naturally gives rise to doubts about how long the competitive advantage presented by a devaluation will persist in the contemporary world. If it tends to dwindle away (as the consequently more rapid inflation gathers force) at about the same time as the effects that a devaluation is normally expected to have upon imports and exports are beginning to show themselves, it is obviously reasonable to express doubts about the usefulness of devaluation in both the short and the longer run—either to improve the current account or, through that means, to stimulate domestic activity.

The efficacy of a devaluation for raising domestic employment may also be reduced, or even negated, if the rise in the price level resulting from a devaluation leads people to try to rebuild their holdings of money and other liquid assets towards their former real level, and so to raise the proportion of their income saved. This would have the effect of dampening domestic demand, in circumstances where this may not be desired. If, on the other hand, the devaluation took place from a position of excess demand, this would be a consideration in favour of it. Certainly, this complication would make the devaluation more likely to improve the current account, because of the resulting decline in domestic activity. But if the aim were to achieve the improvement in the balance of payments by reducing domestic demand, this would have been better achieved by monetary or budgetary measures that would be less likely than would a devaluation to raise the price level or the rate of inflation.

'GLOBAL MONETARISM'

A related strand in the doubts prevalent in recent years about the efficacy of devaluations (or appreciations) for achieving their expected effects on the current account, or on the level of activity, has been the views of so-called 'global monetarists'; to the effect that the world is now so close to being a single market for most commodities that a devaluation is likely before long to raise the price level in the devaluing country by virtually the same proportion as the devaluation.[3] So far as this is true, it means that no devaluation can be effective in improving the current account of the balance of payments or in influencing the level of activity; for in real terms there will then be no effective devaluation, as the price level of the devaluing country will very quickly return to its previous relationship to the price level in the outside world. It would still be open to a country to hold down its price level relative to the rest of the world by taking appropriate budgetary and monetary measures; but a devaluation will not, on this view, have a lasting effect on its *relative* price level. If the global monetarist view is more or less correct, therefore, a devaluation simply raises the price level of the devaluing country; so that a country concerned about its rate of inflation should adopt monetary and budgetary measures that make it possible for it to appreciate; and as this will hold down its rate of inflation to more or less the extent of the appreciation, its competitive position relative to the rest of the world, and so its current account, will not be worsened by the appreciation, nor will its level of activity be reduced.

Very few, if any, economists believe that the adjustment of the domestic price level to a change in the exchange rate could be so quick or so complete as to make the use of the exchange rate wholly ineffective in achieving the 'orthodox' expected effects on trade and the level of activity. But the more fully integrated is the world market for goods and services (the more it operates like a single market), and the more quickly domestic money incomes rise as a result of the price increases that follow a devaluation, the less reliable must a variation in the exchange rate be for achieving the orthodox aims of affecting the current account and the level of activity; and the stronger will be the case for using it, instead, to hold down the country's rate of inflation (at any given level of activity).

One's judgment as to which is the best way to use exchange rate policy therefore depends on whether one feels that the most important direction of causation is from the exchange rate to the price level (as the global monetarists believe—in a very extreme form): or whether, on the contrary, one continues to accept the traditional view that inflation leads to devaluation; in the sense that if a country has more inflation than the rest of the world it will have to devalue (unless, of course, other factors, such as capital flows, move in its favour to an offsetting extent). Clearly, it is useless for a country to devalue in the hope of adjusting for the fact that its rate of inflation has been higher than in other countries if the effect of that devaluation will be simply, or mainly, to raise its price level still further. It is therefore essential for any government that tries to use its exchange rate as a weapon of policy in this sense to be confident that it knows which of the two views is closer to the truth for its own economy. For if a government assumes that it can and should devalue whenever it has suffered a high rate of inflation by world standards, but if it is in fact true that the main effect of devaluation is to raise its rate of inflation still further, it will obviously be unwise for the country to devalue. No-one can reasonably doubt that there is some effect in each direction; that is to say, no-one doubts that a devaluation has some effect in raising the price level of the devaluing country; and, on the other hand, even global monetarists would presumably accept that in the immediate aftermath of a devaluation the price level of the devaluing country does not adjust upwards fully in proportion to the devaluation. The difference of view is therefore about how quickly and how fully the price level will rise after a devaluation—or fall after an appreciation, though some would say the effects may not be symmetrical, in that an appreciation will not be so likely to check inflation as devaluation is to increase it.

It is also partly a matter of whether it is useful to divide the goods and services that a country produces into 'traded' goods and services (whose prices are quickly affected by an alteration in its exchange rate), on the one hand, and 'non-traded' goods and services (which are neither exports nor competing closely with imports, and whose prices therefore do not react quickly to a change in the exchange rate), on the other. It is obviously a matter of degree, in the sense that any particular product may be traded, or at least compete closely with some other item that is, or can be, traded. Even services, which have to be rendered at the point of consumption, are not so obviously 'non-traded' as may appear at first sight—especially now that such large numbers of people travel internationally. The consumer may have a choice between taking a holiday in his own country or taking it overseas. He may often face a choice between attending an entertainment or cultural events in his own country and deciding instead to save his money until he can spend it on similar types of events when he goes abroad; or even deciding, instead of attending a concert, to purchase an imported gramophone record. Even in the case of haircuts (often instanced as a non-traded item par excellence), it is not completely unknown for ladies to travel to another country to have their hair styled; and even men may postpone a hair cut if they are shortly going abroad, and if they believe that they will obtain a better or cheaper cut overseas. In a sense, indeed, all goods and services are in competition to some greater or smaller degree with goods and services traded internationally, and the frontier between the two categories is constantly shifting with prices, incomes and tastes. One should not go so far as to suggest that the distinction is without its usefulness in analysing the effects of exchange rate changes; but one can certainly argue that if a government applies the distinction too rigidly it will underestimate the extent of the price rise that is likely to follow a devaluation.[4]

In short, the closer to the 'global monetarist' end of the spectrum of views one believes the truth to be, and thus the less useful one believes it to be to distinguish between 'traded' and 'non-traded' goods, the more one will doubt whether a government should alter its exchange rate so as to reflect what it believes to be changes in the purchasing power of its currency (that is, in its rate of inflation) compared with that of the rest of the world. But the nearer to the traditionally accepted view about the effects of exchange rates on trade one believes the truth to lie the more confident one would be that a devaluation can be used to improve the current account or to stimulate activity in the devaluing country. (In any case, a country that suffers from rapid inflation, in a world that has generally much lower rates of inflation, is in practice unlikely to be able to avoid devaluation.)

We can, however, reasonably expect that governments are likely to be slow and reluctant to change their long-established views on this matter; so that they are likely to continue to be willing to allow, or to bring about, a depreciation in the hope of improving their balance of trade or reducing unemployment, even when, under present-day conditions, the main effect (perhaps even the sole effect) of doing so may be eventually to raise their price level or their rate of inflation. The risk is, therefore, that they may make excessive use of the exchange rate for the wrong purposes, especially as devaluations tend to be politically popular; for the exporting and import-competing industries that stand to benefit (or think they will benefit) usually have the best organised spokesmen; and the same interests are usually politically strong enough to resist appreciations, even when these would be in the best interests of the consumer or of the country as a whole.

We do not, on the other hand, have to go to the extreme of accepting the global monetarist view, that a depreciation will have none of the normally expected effects on trade, in order to decide appropriate principles for policy. It is, however, prudent to accept the much more moderate view that we cannot nowadays say for sure how far, or how fast, or for how long, a devaluation will improve the current account (or stimulate activity); whereas we can be sure that it will increase the price level, and so the rate of inflation over the relevant period. This means that wherever possible we should *not* use the exchange rate for trying to achieve its traditional purposes, as we have other instruments that can achieve these aims with greater chance of success. But we can certainly say that, whatever effects devaluations or appreciations may have on trade and activity, they will certainly have substantial effects on the price level. If we try to fix the exchange rate at all we should therefore try to fix it at a level that will have helpful effects on the price level. That is to say, if we are troubled by too high a rate of inflation we should be trying to see to it that the exchange rate appreciates, and we should be doing our best to see that it does not depreciate, or that it depreciates as little as possible.

But this does not mean that we should try to fix the exchange rate at an 'unrealistic' figure, if that means building up the country's international reserves to an unnecessarily high level, or allowing them to fall dangerously low. Too often in the past the attempt to maintain or to establish a particular exchange rate has been interpreted as meaning that the reserves should be kept at a figure that would not have been defensible from any other point of view. The fixing of the exchange rate need not, in fact, imply the holding of excessive or inadequate reserves. Both the exchange rate and the level of the reserves might be held at desired levels if the other instruments of policy were adjusted with these aims in view. But, in practice, fixing the exchange rate has often meant that the reserves have been kept at levels that were too high or too low. The maintenance of a particular (undervalued) exchange rate may thus be interpreted (in practice) as justifying a wasteful accumulation of reserves, when the excess could have been better used to buy more imports—and so reduce inflationary pressure—or for increasing foreign aid to other countries; or, on the other hand (if it is overvalued), it may involve reducing the reserves to a point where their level gives rise to speculation against the currency, or where the country is left with an insufficient margin to see it through reasonably forseeable periods of temporary difficulty. If so, the maintenance of the exchange rate at that level by that means is unlikely to be in the country's interests.

Furthermore, if the maintenance of a particular exchange rate involves the country in the imposition of import controls, or other restrictions on its external payments, or in higher tariffs than it would otherwise have chosen; or if it involves operating its economy at a higher or lower level, relative to capacity, than it would otherwise have done: again, this sort of exchange rate policy is highly unlikely to be defensible.

Indeed, the search for the most appropriate exchange rate is somewhat like the search for happiness: it is most likely to be achieved as a byproduct of doing other things well.

This implies that, instead of trying to use the exchange rate as an instrument in itself, a country can best think of the market for foreign exchange as one channel—just as all the other markets in the economy are also channels—through which the most appropriate mix of macroeconomic measures can operate in the process of achieving full employment without inflation. In a closed economy this particular channel is lacking. But an open economy is not fundamentally different from a closed one. It is true that the geographical lines drawn between countries by political considerations give rise to foreign exchange transactions, but the underlying economic realities are not basically changed by the placing of these frontiers. It will be argued in the following section that an open economy will be likely to adopt the most appropriate macroeconomic mix if it applies, so far as possible, basically the same principles as those proposed above as the most appropriate ones in a closed economy. The detailed operation of these measures may be, or at least may appear to be, different in an open economy. But the essential elements are basically the same.

CHOOSING THE APPROPRIATE MIX IN AN OPEN ECONOMY

In an open economy a government has a third objective—the level of its reserves, or the state of its balance of payments—to add to the two that are of concern also in a closed economy (full employment and the avoidance of undue inflation). This external macroeconomic objective is not a complication if the government does not wish to change the reserves or the state of the country's balance of payments, and if it is content to allow the exchange rate to fluctuate (rather than the reserves) according to supply and demand, like any other free market. But it is the setting of all the macroeconomic instruments, and not only the exchange rate, that will determine whether or not the reserves change.

More usually, governments do have a view on whether their reserves are too high or too low; so that we have to accept that governments will usually be trying to raise or lower them, and will therefore have this third macroeconomic objective. We shall therefore discuss below the best choice of measures for raising or lowering the reserves. But we shall assume initially that the level of the reserves is about right, so that the government proposes to allow the effect of any net change in the country's external transactions to be taken by variations in the exchange rate. It will thus be directing its macroeconomic policy towards maintaining the desired level of activity with as little inflation as possible.

If it applies the principles of macroeconomic policy outlined in the earlier chapters for a closed economy, these objectives should be obtainable in an open, as in a closed, economy; but the effects on the exchange rate, and through that channel on the price level and the level of activity, will be important in an open economy.

In outlining the appropriate use of the available measures, it may be helpful to recall the reasons why each of the principal monetary and budgetary measures has different relative effects on the price level and on the level of activity, and to set these considerations in the context of an open economy.

The two sides of the budget—government spending on goods and services, and the level of taxation (together with transfers including subsidies)—have differential effects on the two internal objectives, so far as high tax rates have any degree of cost-push effect (and as some subsidies tend to reduce cost-push). Where this is true, an expansion brought about by increases in government spending will have a greater upward effect on the price level, for a given upward effect on employment, than will a reduction in cost-push taxes having the same effect on activity. This means, in an open economy with an exchange rate that is free to vary, that the same real stimulus given by way of a cut in tax rates can be expected to have a smaller effect in the direction of causing a depreciation in the foreign exchange market than will a rise in government spending having the same effect on domestic activity. It is true that both of these measures will be likely to cause a depreciation, as the country's demand for imports (net of exports) is likely to rise as a result of the rise in its level of activity. But, of these two budgetary weapons, the tax cut alternative will have less upward effect on the price level and so less downward effect on the value of the currency in terms of foreign exchange. As any resulting depreciation will tend to raise the price level, the choice of the tax stimulus will therefore be less inflationary, partly because it will have a smaller downward effect on the exchange rate. It is not really that there is an additional helpful effect in an open economy as a result of choosing the tax cut; but, rather, that there is a different channel through which part of the effect will be felt—provided, of course, that the exchange rate is left free to vary, or that some other measure, such as a tariff cut, is used to ensure that the choice of the less inflationary form of expansion is allowed to have its natural effect through the foreign exchange market, and that it does not lead to a rise in the reserves.

The second differential effect on which the choice of the best mix of macroeconomic weapons was seen to depend in a closed economy was the relative impact on price and output of monetary measures on the one hand and budgetary measures (generally) on the other. In this case, the reason was that a monetary stimulus operates by raising the money supply and reducing interest rates, and this has some direct upward effect on the price level. On the other hand, a purely budgetary measure of expansion (that is, one that does not rely upon the creation of money for providing the stimulus) will be accompanied by an *increase* in interest rates at any given level of activity, to a level higher than under the alternative of the monetary stimulus. A simple way of picturing this is to say that under the purely budgetary stimulus no money is created; so that the price level must naturally be expected to be lower at any given level of activity (with the same available supplies of goods) than under the alternative of a monetary expansion, which operates by increasing the money supply, and so giving people an amount of money, and financial wealth generally, in excess of their normal requirements at the initial price level and level of activity (see Appendix 1).

This means, in an open economy, that the choice of a monetary stimulus will raise the price level by more, and so cause the exchange rate to move correspondingly further in the direction of depreciation, than if the same real stimulus to employment had been given by the less inflationary alternative of a budgetary expansion.

But in the open economy the result of a purchase of bonds by the government may not be solely, and perhaps not mainly, to reduce rates of interest. For if the international flow of capital is sufficiently responsive to changes in relative interest rates, much of the effect of a change of mix in this direction of monetary expansion may well be to reduce the inflow of capital from other countries, as the rates of interest available in the reflating country become less attractive than they would have been if a budgetary measure of expansion had been employed. One would not normally expect the flow of capital to be so responsive to interest rate changes that there would be no fall in interest rates, though that might be so in extreme cases. Normally, therefore, one would expect the bond operations—bond purchases by the government in this case—to have part of their effect through changing asset prices in the country conducting them, and part of their effect through their impact on capital flows, and so on the exchange rate, as these changes in capital flows had their impact on the foreign exchange market. (So far as capital flows are responsive to the level of activity, the two types of policy have the same effects on it. We are here discussing only the difference made to the capital inflow by the choice of measure with which the stimulus is given.)

In the longer run, however, the effect on the exchange rate would be different; for if capital inflow falls (as a result of the reduction in interest rates) in the longer run the payments of interest to other countries will be less than if capital inflow and interest rates had been higher; and at that subsequent stage the effect on the exchange rate will be in the opposite direction to the change that occurred when there were the original effects on the capital account.

The implication in an open economy of the differential effects of monetary and budgetary measures on the price level and on the level of employment is that a country that is trying to minimise its rate of inflation will choose the means of expansion that is least likely to cause a depreciation (or which will be likely to minimise the extent of any depreciation). This means that it will refrain from using monetary measures of expansion, and will stimulate the economy by using budgetary measures, preferably the reduction of cost-push taxes. The choice of a mix to keep interest rates relatively high will also help to strengthen the exchange rate (and so hold down the price level) through capital account transactions.

In addition to the macroeconomic considerations with which we are concerned, a country ought also in any case to consider the general question of whether it is likely to benefit from a capital inflow. In broad principle, if it is to benefit from the capital inflow, the extra resources made available to it as a result of the inflow will have to enable it to increase its output sufficiently to enable it to repay the loan with interest, and still leave it with some net benefit. It may decide to give more weight to the immediate benefits that it will derive from the inflow than to the longer-term costs of the repayment with interest—whether because it expects to be better off (for independent reasons) when the repayments fall due—and so be better placed to bear them; or simply because it is not as concerned about the welfare of posterity as about the welfare of its own generation.

But if we now add the benefit it can obtain from the capital inflow through the contribution it can make to overcoming stagflation, there is obviously a case for a country to have a higher level of capital inflow than would be justifiable in the absence of this consideration.

Of course, if the rest of the world is applying a similar policy mix at the same time, to that extent capital inflow will not be increased. On the other hand, the use of a non-inflationary policy mix in the world generally will benefit all countries; and if the world generally is adopting the same sort of mix there will not be the subsequent problem of interest payments on the extra capital inflow that there is for a country that raises interest rates when the rest of the world is not doing so.

One important extra benefit from adopting a policy mix that will help to restrain inflation in the near future (by attracting more capital inflow) is that the government will consequently normally feel able to operate the economy at nearer to full employment than it would if it had adopted a mix that was causing it to suffer a more rapid rate of inflation. The consequent rise in the level of its output would increase the probability that it will be able to finance the repayment of a given inflow of capital with interest, and still derive a net benefit from the inflow.

It is true that when the interest has to be repaid, this will be an influence operating in the opposite direction; but the downward effect on the rate of inflation may be lasting, if inflationary expectations are held down by the appreciation resulting from the capital inflow. Moreover, even if the repayment of the loan with interest at a later stage resulted in some additions to the rate of inflation at that time, the extra goods and services made possible in the interim by the operation of the economy at nearer to full employment, and the better allocation of resources at each level of activity (resulting from the check to inflation), would leave output permanently higher (especially if any part of the extra resources were devoted to increasing the country's stock of capital, including useful knowledge); so that when the time came to finance these interest payments any consequent stimulus to prices would be offset to some extent by the greater productive potential of the economy.

Even if the capital inflow did not lead the government to operate the economy at nearer to its capacity than it would otherwise have done, the adoption of a mix that would tend to increase capital inflow (lower tax rates and higher interest rates) would, as in a closed economy, tend to increase the level of output and economic welfare at any given level of employment; for if taxes had any undesirable effects on the allocation of resources or on incentives the lower level of tax rates made possible by this mix would itself be a benefit, even if the level of activity were the same.

Furthermore, because this sort of mix would reduce the rate of inflation, it would also reduce the risk that the government might find it hard to keep the level of activity up to the desired level; for, as we saw in Chapter 4, the more inflationary is the policy mix with which a government tries to establish or maintain a given level of activity, the greater the risk of the upward effects of its measures being offset or negated by money wage rises or by increases in the proportion of their income that people save. In an open economy, the additional capital inflow that is made possible by a mix with low taxes and large bond sales is one of the two channels through which these advantages of such a low-tax mix operates; whereas in a closed economy the only channel would be through the lower money supply and the higher nominal interest rates that would presumably exist, at least for a while, until inflation was brought down. But even in an open economy, the effects through the domestic money supply and the market for real and financial assets would also be one channel; for it is highly unlikely that the international flow of capital is so responsive to interest rates that a single country selling bonds will bring about a sufficient rise in its capital inflow to prevent there being any effect on prices in its domestic markets for goods and financial assets or any fall in its money supply.

Direct Capital Inflow

A country may not wish there to be an increase in the scale of direct investment in its industries from overseas, especially by multinational companies. But this is quite a different matter from the question of total net capital inflow. For net capital inflow can be affected also by borrowing by domestically controlled firms and by individuals, as well as borrowing by the government, and also by changes in capital outflow, including leads and lags on current account payments. Moreover, multinational companies can increase the scale of their operations in a country without bringing in more capital (for they may borrow within the host country). In any event, a host country's policies towards direct investment from overseas should be implemented by appropriate taxes or laws to control it in the appropriate sense, where there is a valid case for wishing to influence the scale, form and direction of direct investment. It should not be confused with the macroeconomic policy issues relating to the overall state of the capital account. If the adoption of a more appropriate policy mix makes possible a higher level of activity, however, the additional capital inflow required as a result of such a policy may well be at least partly in the form of a higher level of direct investment than might otherwise have been felt desirable. For the higher rate of economic growth that should result from a better policy mix should make a higher level of direct investment both more probable and more likely to benefit the host country. Furthermore, if the rise in capital inflow can be most readily and most beneficially obtained from this source the host country is unlikely to find it advantageous to deny itself this sort of inflow, if ready access to it facilitates the implementation of a less inflationary mix and a higher level of activity.

BORROWING IN AN OPEN ECONOMY: THE INTERESTS OF POSTERITY

We saw in Chapter 5 that the choice of a mix involving a high level of government borrowing and a correspondingly lower level of taxation may involve posterity in a higher level of taxation, and correspondingly more cost-push inflation, than it would otherwise have suffered. If, however, the change of mix towards bond-financing enables the government to operate the economy at a higher level of activity (relative to capacity) than it would have felt desirable if it had not adopted this less inflationary policy mix, posterity also may be expected to benefit—provided only that some of the extra output that then becomes available is used to make possible a higher level of investment than would otherwise have occurred. Posterity could still lose on balance, however, if this benefit fell short of the social costs inflicted on it by the need for it to impose a higher level of taxation (or to have a lower level of government spending) than it would otherwise have felt to be desirable.

In an open economy, essentially the same principles apply, except that some of the higher level of interest payments made as a result of the shift towards bond-financing will normally be made to residents of other countries, and some of the downward effect on the price level occurring in the near future as a result of the higher level of government borrowing will be attributable to the extra resources being made available to the country as a result of the higher capital inflow. For an open economy whose government decides to borrow more and tax less, the scope for an immediate reduction in the price level or the rate of inflation is greater than in an otherwise similar closed economy, as the open economy has available to it the possibility of overseas borrowing to increase the amount of real resources available to it (at any level of activity) with which to hold down the rate of inflation in the near future. But, on the other hand, in subsequent years the resources available to it will be correspondingly reduced by the amount of foreign exchange it has to pay out by way of interest and for debt repayments. In a closed economy, the only cost is that which may be inflicted on posterity as a result of its having to impose taxes that would not otherwise have been necessary (or to forego government spending that would otherwise have been thought desirable). In an open economy also these costs will have to be borne; but, in addition, in the open economy posterity will have to accept the cost of making the transfers of interest, profits and debt repayments to residents of other countries.

The immediate scope for a country to benefit from using a higher level of net government borrowing to check inflation, and also the ultimate costs of doing so, are thus both greater in an open than in a closed economy. But the basic choice facing an open economy is in principle the same as in a closed economy. In each case the government has to weigh the benefit to the present generation (or to itself in terms of electoral popularity) against its own evaluation of any costs it may be imposing on posterity. If the shift of mix in a less inflationary direction had no upward effect on the total resources available to posterity, one might feel bound to urge a government to exercise great caution about shifting the mix in the proposed direction (provided, of course, that it was already pitching the level of its borrowing from the public and from overseas at what would be the ideal level from other points of view). But if the government feels able and willing to operate the economy at nearer to its capacity as a result of adopting a mix that will help to hold down prices, posterity will also benefit by having thus made available to it a larger volume of real resources, as the country's capital stock should be greater, provided that some part of the extra output is devoted to investment. As the prolonged stagflation that results from governments trying to restrain inflation by permitting unemployment is likely to have the effect of prolonged stagnation of the level of investment, a shift of the policy mix in the less inflationary direction seems certain to increase the capital stock, and so to benefit posterity considerably on that account. One might also argue that the longer inflation—or stagflation—is permitted to continue, the harder will it be for posterity to stop it, as expectations of continued inflation, or stagflation (and even public and governmental tolerance of them), are likely to become harder to reverse as time goes on. If these considerations are given their proper weight, therefore, it is unconvincing to argue that a government ought to be seriously inhibited from shifting the mix towards bond-financing and away from tax-financing merely on account of tenderness towards the interests of posterity. As in a closed economy, one of the best things the government of an open economy can do for posterity is to stop stagflation—and in an open economy this may involve borrowing more from overseas than would otherwise have been advisable; and using the proceeds of the additional borrowing to make possible a higher level of imports at any given level of activity, and also to make possible a higher level of activity than would otherwise have been feasible at a given price level or rate of inflation.

THE APPROPRIATE MACROECONOMIC MIX FOR VARIOUS SITUATIONS

In the light of these considerations that affect the comparative advantage of the various monetary and budgetary instruments for achieving the different macroeconomic objectives in an open economy, let us consider the most appropriate ways of choosing how to vary them so as to achieve the desired level of activity, the desired state of the balance of payments, and the desired rate of inflation. We do not know the exact relative effect of each instrument on each of these objectives, so that we cannot in fact set each of them at the level that would give the best approximation to achieving simultaneously all these objectives. But as we know at least something about the relative strengths of the principal weapons in achieving each of these objectives, we can outline the principles on which they should be varied with an eye to achieving these various aims—or at least for refraining from changing them in directions that will take the economy further away from these goals.

As the main contemporary problem is to find the appropriate mix for dealing with stagflation (less than full employment together with an undesirably rapid rise in the price level), we shall first outline the appropriate mix for dealing with this problem in an open economy, under alternative assumptions about the state of its balance of payments.

Stagflation with External Balance

If the reserves and the balance of payments are in a satisfactory state, so that the government is not trying to change them, it can leave the exchange rate free to adjust to demand and supply, without any intervention in the foreign exchange market (as intervention means adding to or subtracting from the reserves).

The principles in this case are the same as in a closed economy. So long as the level of unemployment (and inflation) is too high, the best instrument for stimulating activity is tax cuts; and so long as inflation is too rapid the best way of correcting it is by the sale of bonds to the public; that is, by a tightening of monetary policy. The choice of tax cuts as the means of stimulus will minimise any upward effect of the stimulus on the price level. The bond sales will also tend to reduce domestic inflation; and, in addition, in an open economy the tight monetary policy will tend to improve the capital account, and so to cause the exchange rate to appreciate. A sufficient movement of the mix in this direction could offset the tendency towards depreciation that would otherwise result from the stimulus to activity.

Stagflation and Low Reserves

If a country suffering from stagflation wishes to raise the level of its reserves, it should use its monetary policy with this aim in mind, tightening it until it brings about the desired improvement in its reserves, whilst offsetting the undesired downward effect on domestic activity that such a tightening of monetary policy would otherwise have, by making its budgetary policy correspondingly more expansionary. So long as it is worried by cost-push inflation its preference should again be for implementing this expansionary budgetary policy mainly by cutting cost-push taxes (or by paying cost-reducing subsidies). The only difference between the first case and this one would be that the tightening of monetary policy would have to be taken to the point where the reserves rose to the desired extent; and the resulting improvement in the balance of payments would up to that point have to be allowed to raise the reserves, rather than to cause an appreciation. This means that the downward effect on the domestic price level that was obtained in the first case by the appreciation will to that extent not be available in this second case; so that the cutting of cost-push taxes would here be the only instrument working to correct this.

Stagflation with High Reserves

On the other hand, if the country suffering from stagflation has excessive reserves, it could and should use the excess to obtain an increase in the supply of goods, by changing the general setting of its policy instruments in such a way as to worsen its current account, and perhaps also to reduce net capital inflow. It could more safely expand the level of activity than in either of the first two cases, provided that it took steps to ensure that a rise in imports (or a reduction in exports) took place; for this would lead to an increase in the supply of goods available in the economy as demand rose, and so hold down the rate of inflation at any given level of activity. The best policy would be a tax cut, as this would have helpful effects (in this situation) on all the macroeconomic objectives—output, the reserves, and the rate of inflation. An appreciation or a tariff cut would be an appropriate way of using the reserves, but would itself reduce demand and activity. The use of an easier monetary policy to reduce the reserves could also provide some of the desired expansionary effect, but would increase the rate of inflation.

Excess Demand

If a country is not troubled by stagflation, the essentials of the solution to any problems can be found by an appropriate adaptation of the principles already outlined. If it is in a situation of excess demand and wishes to reduce the rate of inflation as rapidly as possible, it should reduce the excess demand by tightening its monetary policy, or, as a second choice, by reducing government spending, as these measures will have a greater downward effect on the price level than would an increase in taxes, because of the cost-push effects of taxation. It is conceivable that a country might feel that the level of demand was too high for its available capacity, but that the rate of inflation was not serious, in which case it might be less desirable for it to concentrate its disinflationary measures on tighter monetary policy or on reducing government spending and it might be more justified in raising taxes. But the underlying principle would be the same as in a closed economy and in the case of stagflation already considered; the best approach would be to vary its monetary policy with an eye primarily to restraining inflation, and if that did not reduce the level of effective demand sufficiently, to use changes (in this case cuts) in government spending with an eye to affecting the level of demand, and to raise its tax rates only so long as it was not concerned about the rate of inflation.

If a country suffering from excess demand is also worried that its reserves are inadequate, the case for it to tighten its monetary policy will be correspondingly stronger as this has a more pronounced upward effect on the reserves—partly because of the additional impetus that it would give to capital inflow (for a given effect in reducing activity) than either of the budgetary measures. (Again, therefore, variations in monetary policy are best made primarily with an eye to the objective of external balance.) By the same token, therefore, if its reserves are too high it should be prepared to adopt expansionary monetary measures, and to correct any undesired upward effect this has on the level of activity by appropriately tighter budgetary measures—restraint in government spending to cut domestic demand, along with tax increases if it is not worried about cost-push inflation (but tax reductions if this is a problem). In these circumstances, a tariff cut or an appreciation could normally be expected to operate in the appropriate direction on all targets.

Full Employment with Inflation

Intermediate between these poles of macroeconomic misery, we may have cases of countries which are satisfied with one aspect of their internal macroeconomic situation, but which are worried about the other. One such case would be a country which has what it regards as about the right level of activity, but too rapid a rate of inflation. If such a country follows the principles already given, it will cut its tax rates (or pay cost-reducing subsidies) to reduce its cost-push inflation, and correct any undesired upward effect this may have on activity either by bond sales (a tightening of monetary policy) or by restraint in government spending. If it were simultaneously concerned that its reserves were inadequate it would prefer to tighten monetary policy (again, following the principle of gearing its monetary policy to the state of the reserves). But if its reserves were considered excessive it could pursue a more expansionary monetary policy, which would tend to reduce them, both through discouraging capital inflow and through raising the domestic price level. It should continue to cut taxes so long as inflation was too rapid, and if that, too, gave an undue stimulus to domestic activity, this effect would require to be offset by a correspondingly greater restraint in government spending.

Recession with Price Stability

In the case of a country which does not consider its rate of inflation excessive, but which has less than full employment, the stimulus should be given by one of the budgetary weapons if it is not worried about the level of its reserves. If, however, there were excessive reserves it should be more inclined to raise government spending than to cut taxes. A monetary expansion would reduce the reserves still more quickly, though with greater likelihood of raising the rate of inflation to a point where it might become unacceptable. This suggests a need for at least partial reliance upon tax cuts for providing the required stimulus.

Summary of Principles

It has seemed worthwhile to describe the application of the suggested principles to the various combinations of macroeconomic problems that a country may face. But the basic principles are the same in each case.[5]

First, if the country is satisfied with the level of reserves and is therefore prepared to let the exchange rate (rather than the reserves) reflect any change in its external transactions, it should apply the same principles as those suggested in earlier chapters for the closed economy. That is, it should cut tax rates when it has less than full employment and when inflation is also high; and it should tighten monetary policy while inflation is too rapid.

Secondly, if it is concerned to bring about a change in the level of the reserves, as well as to achieve the best approximation to the two internal objectives, it should direct the variations in its monetary policy primarily to achieving the desired change in its reserves, tightening monetary policy when the reserves are too low and easing it when they are too high. If the resulting change in the internal situation will push the economy further away from full employment or from the desired rate of inflation, it should correct this by directing changes in its tax rates primarily towards minimising inflation, reducing taxes (or paying additional cost-reducing subsidies) so long as this sort of inflation is too rapid, and correcting any undesired effects this may have on the level of activity by adjusting its remaining weapon of government spending.

It is true that these various measures may work towards their objectives at varying speeds, and with different lags; and if one knows enough about the speed with which they each affect the main elements in the situation one will vary their rate of adjustment accordingly. But the problems that are presented by such difficulties as these are likely to be minor beside those that will arise if a government tries to vary its macroeconomic measures in the 'wrong' ways; that is to say, if it varies each of them with an eye to affecting macroeconomic objectives other than those with which the weapon in question is best equipped to deal.

One could illustrate this by taking the case of a country suffering from stagflation and a balance of payments deficit. It ought to tighten monetary policy (in order to improve its balance of payments and incidentally also to help check inflation), whilst cutting taxes in order to check cost-push inflation and to stimulate demand. If, instead, it tries to stimulate domestic demand by means of an expansionary monetary policy, it will make its balance of payments worse and this effect will be greater than if it had given the stimulus by a budgetary expansion, especially a tax cut. If it then reacts to the worsening of its balance of payments by tightening its budgetary policy (especially if this takes the form of increasing taxes), this method of correcting the worsening of the balance of payments will move the economy further away from the output and inflation targets than it was initially. If it continues to vary the setting of each of these instruments with an eye to affecting the 'wrong' objective the situation will move further and further away from the desired goals.

IMPLICATIONS OF CHANGES IN THE DEMAND FOR AND SUPPLY OF MONEY

The previous section discussed the implications for the macroeconomic mix of the relative effects of monetary and budgetary measures on interest rates, and so on capital inflow, and their respective effects on the price level. The different macroeconomic measures operate partly by having different effects on the relationship between the demand and supply of money at any given level of activity, and the choice of mix may also affect the exchange rate through this channel.[6]

As activity increases there will naturally be a rise in the demand for money; and if the stimulus is one that involves a reduction in the rate of interest the rise in the demand for money (for any given real stimulus) will be greater. The stimulus that has the greatest upward effect on the price level will also (other things being equal) naturally have a greater upward effect on the demand for money.

A monetary measure of expansion is, of course, caused by an increase in the money supply relative to the demand for it, whereas a purely budgetary measure does not involve any rise in the money supply. A monetary measure of expansion is therefore normally associated with a fall in interest rates in a closed economy; which means that the extra money created drives interest rates down as well as expanding activity. In an open economy, therefore, it is equally natural to assume (as has been done so far in our analysis for an open economy) that the choice of a monetary measure of expansion will cause interest rates to fall, and net capital outflow will therefore tend to increase (or net capital inflow to fall).

But, as we saw in Chapter 5, it is possible that the increase in the demand for money as income rises may be so great that even a monetary stimulus may lead eventually to a rise in interest rates (see Chapter 5, page 101). If the extra demand for money is so great as to exceed the injection of money that provided the stimulus, the consequent rise in interest rates will, therefore, in an open economy have some effect in the direction of increasing net capital inflow (or reducing net outflow). Although this is unlikely, it is possible that if this effect were great enough, it could even exceed the adverse effect on the current account resulting from the rise in activity, and so cause an actual rise in the reserves under fixed exchange rates, or an appreciation under flexible rates, even if it were a monetary stimulus that was chosen.

In any event, even if one takes into account the extra demand for money balances that results from a rise in activity, the case made above for choosing to give any desired stimulus by budgetary, rather than monetary, measures in a stagflationary open economy is not altered; for even with this response the rise in interest rates, and any consequent appreciation, will be that much larger with a budgetary expansion.

If a purely budgetary measure of expansion is chosen—that is, one that does not involve a rise in the money supply—under fixed exchange rates, the extra demand for money will be met by an improvement in the overall balance of payments; that is, by a rise in the reserves, as a result of some combination of a stronger current account (as people reduce their total spending out of a given income in an effort to build up their money balances), and a stronger capital account (as people borrow more or lend less overseas).

If the exchange rate is freely flexible, however, the reserves cannot rise, so that this means of meeting the demand for extra money balances is not available. The same measures to reduce inflation at a given level of activity and to improve the capital account will now tend to cause an appreciation. The reduction of the price level resulting from the appreciation will make the (given) level of the money supply able to support a higher real level of activity.

At the same time, so far as the level of interest rates in the country under discussion is free to rise above that in the rest of the world, it may be expected to increase—under either fixed or floating exchange rates—as a result of the budgetary stimulus, and that will lead people to economise in their holdings of money balances at each level of money income. This is therefore another route through which the extra demand for money balances is likely to be met.

The upshot of introducing this consideration of the demand for money balances is to reach our earlier conclusions in another way. The choice of a purely budgetary measure of expansion must be expected to lead to less depreciation, or more appreciation, and therefore to some downward effect on the price level, by comparison with a monetary measure having the same upward effect on the level of activity. For a purely budgetary measure would not involve the creation of any of the extra money required to meet the rise in demand for money at the higher level of activity.

GOVERNMENT SPENDING AND TAX RATES

We have now to consider whether similar factors also alter the balance of advantage as between the two budgetary instruments—a rise in government spending and a reduction in cost-push taxes.

The effect of the reduction in cost-push taxes will be to improve the current account, and so to cause less depreciation (at any given level of activity) by comparison with an equivalent stimulus provided by an increase in government spending. On the other hand, the lower level of prices resulting from a reduction in cost-push taxes (compared with other types of expansionary measures) will in effect increase the real money supply (for any given nominal money supply). There will not, therefore, be so much inducement for people to try to build up their money holdings by borrowing more (or lending less) overseas. This means that there will not be so much appreciation through capital account transactions as one could expect from a similar stimulus given by a rise in government spending on goods and services. If the tax cut therefore resulted in very much less capital inflow, the exchange rate would consequently be weaker in this case, so far as it depended on capital account transactions. If, however, international capital mobility was not great, the effects through the current account would dominate, so that a tax cut would (taking current and capital transactions together) make for a stronger exchange rate than the alternative of a rise in government spending. But it is not possible to say for sure that the effects through the current account will exceed those operating in the direction of appreciation through the capital account.

Long-run Aspects

In the short run, the mix most likely to hold down the price level at a given level of activity (in an open as in a closed economy) will, as we have seen, be one involving a low money supply and low tax rates. But in the longer run, when the consequent rise in net payments of interest and dividends to other countries comes to outweigh the helpful effects on the exchange rate of the rise in net capital inflow resulting from such a mix, this is no longer certain. For the ultimate outcome will depend on whether this rise in net interest payments has a greater downward effect on the exchange rate than the upward effect resulting from the reduction in the price level due to the internal effects of adopting this mix.

If the capital flows are not very responsive to interest rates, a mix involving tight money and fiscal ease will be desirable in both the short and longer run. But the greater the responsiveness of capital flows to changes in interest rates, the greater the extent to which the helpful effect on the exchange rate (and so on the price level) will be concentrated into the short run—while capital flows are being affected—whilst the longer-run benefit will be correspondingly less.

Of the two budgetary measures, the choice of a tax cut might reduce capital inflow (by comparison with that which would result from a rise in government spending) sufficiently to offset its relatively favourable effects through the current account in the short run; for, with a tax cut, the price level, and so the demand for money, will be lower. But in the long run, when net interest payments to other countries will therefore be lower if the tax-cut alternative is chosen, its undoubted effect in holding down the price level at any given level of activity will mean that the exchange rate will be stronger, and the price level lower, if the tax cut is the alternative chosen.

The Macro Mix in the Short Run under Floating Rates

If the capital account reacts to a change in macroeconomic policy more quickly than does the level of activity and the current account, this may raise special difficulties. Under a freely floating exchange rate a measure of monetary expansion would then reduce net capital inflow and so cause a depreciation and a rise in the price level (or rate of inflation), without stimulating activity or improving the state of the current account in the short run. On the other hand, a measure of budgetary expansion will tend to raise interest rates, and so increase capital inflow (at any given level of activity), so that the exchange rate appreciates; and this will dampen the expansionary effect on the country taking the measure, whilst spreading a large part of the expansionary effect to other countries.

If the country taking the expansionary measures could be sure whether the main effects would be on the capital account (and, if so, for how long), it could select a mix of monetary and budgetary measures that provided the desired net stimulus to activity without changing relative interest rates, and so without having the effect on the exchange rate through the capital account that might either (with a monetary expansion) cause more inflation without giving a real stimulus or (in the case of a budgetary stimulus) cause most or all of the immediate expansionary effect to be felt in other countries. It would, in principle, be possible to choose to adopt expansionary budgetary measures which, taken alone, would have tended to raise interest rates, but simultaneously to have a sufficiently expansionary monetary policy to ensure that interest rates did not rise. As domestic activity began to respond to the stimulus it would become appropriate to move towards the mix of measures that would have been chosen if this complication (of a faster reaction of the capital account than of employment and the current account) had not been present.[7] (As we have seen in earlier sections, for a stagflationary economy this would involve giving as much of the stimulus as possible by budgetary measures, preferably tax cuts.)

If the stimulus were given by tax cuts, and these had any effect in holding down the price level (at any given level of activity), interest rates would not rise so much in the country adopting the measure as they would if it had relied on an expansion in government spending. For the demand for money, and so interest rates, will not rise so much (for any given real stimulus) if the stimulus is given by a cut in cost-push taxes. The introduction of this complication therefore constitutes an additional argument for giving a stimulus by way of a tax cut (at least so long as it is difficult for a government to assess in advance how far effects operating through the capital account of the balance payments will precede the effects on domestic activity and on the current account).

THE IMPLICATIONS OF A PERVERSE REACTION OF DEMAND TO CHANGES IN INTEREST RATES

We saw in the analysis of a closed economy that if a government follows the suggested principles of varying the policy mix, the same principles will also be appropriate if it should happen that the level of demand is increased when the government takes measures by way of monetary policy that tend to raise interest rates (see Chapter 4, page 75). So far in our analysis of the open economy we have made the usual assumption that a tighter monetary policy will depress activity (other things being equal). But it is worth considering whether the proposed principles for the use of the macroeconomic instruments will be appropriate even if this is not so.

Just as in the case of a closed economy, the suggested mix would work even if a sale of bonds, and the consequent rise in interest rates, had some effect in stimulating activity. But in the open economy it will naturally work partly through the exchange rate (or through any other measures, such as changes in tariffs or import controls, that ensure that the level of reserves does not change as a result). If the country is troubled by stagflation, a tightening of monetary policy with the aim of reducing the price level will in this case tend also to stimulate activity, so far as interest rates are in fact raised. On the other hand, if the effect is partly to attract more capital inflow (or to reduce outflow) this will tend to make the exchange rate appreciate and thus to hold down the price level; but so far as it is through this route of extra capital inflow that it exerts its effects of holding down prices there will not be a rise in domestic interest rates, so that the upward effect that a rise in interest rates would have had on domestic activity (on our present assumptions) will to that extent not materialise. Any upward effect on demand that does eventuate will obviously be helpful, however, if we are starting from a state of stagflation; and if budgetary policy (preferably a cut in tax rates) is being varied with an eye to maintaining full employment, the net stimulus required from this source to maintain a given level of demand will thus be less than would otherwise have been required. The proposed mix of measures will therefore also work in an open economy that reacts in this unexpected, and presumably normally unlikely, way. (But, as we saw in Chapter 5, it is by no means impossible that such a reaction may occur in a situation of stagflation.)

On the other hand, if the government is misguided enough not to adopt the proposed mix, deciding instead to adopt a monetary policy that holds down interest rates in the hope of stimulating activity, it would in fact thereby depress activity still further—if output responds in this 'perverse' way to interest rate changes. At the same time, it would be bringing about more inflation (or a higher price level) at any given level of activity than if it had used its macroeconomic instruments in an appropriate manner. For its tax rates—and so cost-push inflation from this source—will be higher than if it had provided a stimulus by reducing them instead of adopting such an 'expansionary' monetary policy. At the same time, the 'expansionary' monetary policy will be operating partly by holding down domestic interest rates; and so far as it therefore tends to reduce capital inflow (and to cause capital outflow) it will be making the exchange rate depreciate, and so causing a rise in the price level from that source. So long as the government reacts to such a situation by continuing to adopt a tight budgetary policy (especially if it keeps taxes high instead of reducing them), whilst failing to tighten monetary policy sufficiently, it will therefore be helping to intensify both unemployment and inflation. Once again (as in the case of the closed economy), it should be stressed that we cannot normally say for certain in any given economy whether activity might respond perversely to changes in interest rates: but the risk that, if that were so, the wrong sort of mix could lead to a continuously worsening stagflation should be a powerful supplementary argument for a government to adopt a more appropriate assignment of instruments to objectives; especially as the right use of these main macroeconomic measures will be in principle the same as in the 'orthodox' situation (where a tightening of monetary policy would be expected to depress the level of demand).

Effects of Exchange Rate Changes on Activity

The view taken in the foregoing analysis has been that the effects of exchange rate changes on activity and on the current account (in real terms, or in terms of foreign exchange) are so uncertain that governments should not try to use alterations in the exchange rate for affecting these aims of macroeconomic policy. In any event, experience has shown that once governments try to fix a particular exchange rate this usually becomes an aim in itself, and thus often prejudices the possibility of achieving the real aims of macroeconomic policy. The exchange rate certainly affects the price level and the rate of inflation; so that if it is being varied consciously, this objective of policy should be the principal target at which exchange rate alterations should aim. But the view has been taken above that a preferable approach is not to think of the exchange rate as an instrument of policy at all, but simply as one channel through which the mix of monetary and budgetary instruments will operate in an open economy; so that if the mix adopted is one having little or no upward effect on the price level, the exchange rate will appreciate by more (or depreciate by less) than if a more inflationary mix had been chosen.

If it has, nevertheless, to be accepted that governments will not leave the exchange rate free to find its own level, it is important for them to give close attention to its likely effects on all of the objectives of macroeconomic policy. If they try to keep the exchange rate as strong as possible, in order to use it with the aim of restraining inflation, they will want to know whether or not this will tend to depress domestic activity. If, on the other hand, they are tempted to bring about a devaluation, despite its upward effects on the price level, they will need to be confident that this will have helpful effects in the direction of improving the balance of payments or the level of activity.

The objection that most governments (and industries) are likely to have to the use of an appreciation for the purpose of restraining inflation is the expectation that this will depress activity and worsen the current account. But it is by no means certain that this will be the result, especially under present-day conditions, when the price effects of an alteration in the exchange rate quickly spread to the internal price level and to money wage rates.

The principal effects of an appreciation are as follows:

1. It will tend to reduce the prices (in terms of the appreciating country's currency) of both exports and imports. Where the traders concerned are to some extent in a monopoly position, however, they may not pass on to consumers the whole of these potential price reductions, at least in the short run. If they do not, the downward effects on domestic activity that can normally be expected, as a result of the stimulus to imports, and of the diversion of resources from exporting to meeting the demands of the home market, may be correspondingly weakened or delayed.

2. When and if the prices of traded goods (exports, imports, and close substitutes for imports) in the appreciating country are reduced, this may have the effect of reducing the output of those industries producing exports and of those industries competing with imports.

3. Those industries that make considerable use of imported materials, components or capital goods will find their costs reduced, and are to that extent likely to increase their output.

4. So far as output is reduced over the economy as a whole, this will tend to reduce the level of real demand and employment, not only in the industries directly affected but also in those whose sales are reduced by any reduction there may be in the expenditure of those who would otherwise have been employed in the industries adversely affected by the appreciation.

5. As the general price level (and probably also the rise in money wage rates) will to some extent be reduced by the appreciation, this may even act as a stimulus to activity. One way in which this may occur is as a result of the consequent rise in the real value of people's money balances, and in the real value of any other assets they hold that are fixed in money terms (such as government bonds). This may lead them to consider these assets to be now excessive, and therefore to increase their spending on goods and services. Another way in which it might occur is if the business world had hitherto been inhibited from investing as a result of a high rate of inflation, and of the uncertainties about future profitability to which it gave rise, or by a rapid rise in money wage-rates.

It may be seen that not all these effects on activity are in the same direction. The price level may be expected to fall, but it is not certain whether the net effect on activity will be upwards or downwards.

The more extensively, and the more immediately, the price level in the appreciating country is affected by the prices of goods and services in the rest of the world, the more likely is it that an appreciation will not reduce the level of domestic activity or worsen the current account of the balance of payments (in terms of foreign exchange), but simply hold down the price level in the appreciating country. This being so, a government that decides to use an appreciation to restrain inflation will not necessarily have to take steps to introduce much by way of expansionary measures to maintain a given level of activity after an appreciation; and it is possible that it might even have to make the setting of its monetary and budgetary measures less expansionary in order to prevent a rise in demand. In the same way, if it starts from a situation of stagflation, it is possible that appreciation may not only help to restrain inflation but may also actually raise the level of activity; in which case correspondingly less will be required by way of tax cuts to bring the economy back to full employment.

The normal expectation would, however, be that some stimulatory action will be required (in order to maintain a given level of activity) after an appreciation; and if the rate of inflation is considered excessive this can best be done by way of tax cuts. If there are also fears that the appreciation will lead to a deterioration in the current account, some tightening of monetary policy will also be desirable in order to have a favourable effect on capital inflow. Any downward effect on domestic activity that results from the tightening of monetary policy should naturally be offset by further cuts in cost-push taxes.

If, however, it should happen that an appreciation actually stimulates activity, an economy that starts from a situation of stagflation will find that the application of the policies already suggested will not come amiss. For the tax cuts will combine with the appreciation to check inflation (at any given level of activity) and will in this case also combine with them in the direction of stimulating activity. If the appreciation actually improves the state of the current account, provided that monetary policy continues to be directed towards the state of the balance of payments, it will not in this case need to be tightened (or not so much as it would if appreciation worsened the current account). In other words, in this perverse case an appreciation will help to overcome stagflation in both its aspects, whereas devaluation will make it worse. As devaluation will always make inflation worse, a country suffering from stagflation will be very unwise to try to use a devaluation as a means of overcoming its problems, if it can be avoided.

Effects on the Exchange Rate through Expectations

Even if the changes in the pattern of trade that occur as a result of a devaluation are slow to show themselves, the expectation that they will eventually come to pass is likely to lead to additional inflows of capital to the devaluing country even well in advance of the effects on trade. But if there are doubts about the efficacy of devaluation for achieving its normal purposes these anticipatory capital flows are correspondingly less likely to occur. If, however, a government shows by the adoption of non-inflationary policy mixes that it is capable of maintaining high levels of activity by means that do not have much (if any) upward effect upon the price level and on wage levels, and that it is therefore likely to continue to maintain activity, this is likely to have an especially favourable effect on capital inflows, not only because real post-tax returns to lenders are likely to be relatively high, but also because the growth prospects for the country concerned, and the probable strength of its currency, will be making it an attractive place in which to invest for these reasons also. Expectational effects operating on the exchange rate through capital flows are therefore likely to reinforce the successful, or prospectively successful, introduction of a non-inflationary policy mix in an open economy.

Two Simultaneous Perversities

We have considered the possibility that an appreciation might stimulate activity. We have also considered the possibility that a rise in interest rates might stimulate demand. In each of these cases we have seen that if the normal policy prescriptions suggested above are followed, no serious difficulties for policy-makers should arise—and that the penalty for adopting the wrong sort of policy mix will be correspondingly greater if either of these contingencies occurred.

We must now say something about the (presumably still more remote) possibility that both of these situations might occur simultaneously.

If a rise in interest rates stimulated activity, its effects on the balance of payments would be correspondingly less favourable;

so that if the exchange rate were free to vary, this would mean that a rise in interest rates would be less likely to cause an appreciation and more likely to lead to a depreciation. If at the same time a depreciation tended to reduce demand, the adoption of a tight monetary policy would thus be more likely to depress activity than if the orthodox assumption held good (that appreciations tend to depress activity and depreciations to stimulate it). There would thus be more need to adopt expansionary budgetary measures if the initial situation was one of stagflation (and correspondingly less need to adopt a contractionary budget if the problem were excess demand). But, again, provided the setting of the budget is being varied in the light of the state of domestic activity, the existence of simultaneously perverse effects of both interest rates and exchange rates need not give rise to serious problems. For appreciations and increases in interest rates would then be contributing to overcoming both inflation and unemployment—on these unorthodox assumptions. But, again, if both of these unorthodox situations prevailed, a government that tried to use an expansionary monetary policy or a devaluation to stimulate activity could fall into serious difficulties; for both of these measures would not only tend to raise the price level but also to make unemployment worse. If then—in contrast to the policy recommended here—it proceeded to adopt a contractionary budget in the hope of thereby reducing inflation or of improving the balance of payments, it would drive activity down still further in the process of trying to achieve that aim.

In short, provided that a government pursues what has been proposed above as a sound macroeconomic mix, it need not be concerned about the possibility that the level of activity may react perversely to a change in interest rates or in the exchange rate, or both. But in either of these cases the penalty—by way of the unintentional perpetuation of stagflation—for adopting a misguided policy mix will be even greater than in the normal situation.

MORE SPECIFIC CHANGES OF BUDGETARY INSTRUMENTS

We have so far considered only general changes in monetary or budgetary instruments as a means of improving the balance of payments at a given level of activity. But if a sharp improvement of the balance of payments is required, it may be worth considering measures of budgetary policy more directly related to differentiating between domestic and external payments.

One measure that has been used by various governments is the reduction or elimination of value-added tax (VAT) upon exports. This appears to have been accepted (at least by a wide range of countries) as being consistent with international commitments not to subsidise exports.

There are other fiscal instruments that could come into the same category. One would be the reduction of any indirect taxes paid on the purchase of home-produced goods and services (while taxes were still being levied on comparable imported products). The deficiency of such a device is that it would tend also to attract resources away from exporting towards supplying the home market, though for a country with ample spare resources this consideration would probably not be important. Moreover, as the resources would be replacing imports, they would in any event be going into activities that would tend to improve the balance of payments.

A similar effect would be obtained by subsidising the domestic production of any items that would replace imports. But it would be hard or impossible to decide which goods and services would be likely to replace imports most economically and efficiently; the only argument for adopting this approach would be if the superior alternative of subsidising domestic production generally were felt to involve (in some sense) too high a level of government expenditure. If import-replacing production only was subsidised, however, there would again be a risk of such a policy pulling resources away from the production of exports; though, again, if there were ample spare resources in the economy this would be less likely. In either case, if the payment of the subsidies would otherwise have had unwanted upward effects on activity, those effects could and should be offset by either reductions in government spending on goods and services or by increased borrowing from the public.

The more general was the coverage of any subsidy granted to both import-replacing production and to exports, the more closely would the effects approximate to those of a devaluation in terms of their effects on the relative attractiveness to domestic producers of producing for export markets, rather than catering for those home demands that would otherwise be satisfied by imported goods and services. It is true that a devaluation is in some ways like a flat-rate subsidy both on exports and on those home products that compete with imported goods and services. But an important difference would be that a subsidy—or a reduction of cost-push taxation—on the same production (for exports and for import-saving production) would operate in a way that would tend to hold down the domestic price level at any given level of activity, provided that its monetary effects were sufficiently offset by either reductions in government spending on goods and services or (preferably in terms of its effects on the price level) by increased sales of bonds to the non-bank public. As this cost-reducing mix would not operate in a way that raised the price level (at the given level of activity), but, rather, would tend to reduce it, it would not elicit an upward response of wages and prices that would tend to undo its effects on the current account; whereas, as we have seen, a devaluation does suffer from that disadvantage.

A Flat-rate Subsidy on Inputs, Compared with a Devaluation

So far as the purpose of a devaluation is to make domestic firms better able to compete with imported products, and to export at competitive prices, a flat-rate subsidy or a tax-cut that holds down the costs of production of businesses should, as we have just seen, be able to fulfil the same purpose as a devaluation. But the subsidies or tax cuts will tend to stimulate real demand, whereas a devaluation may be more likely to cut real consumption, by raising the prices of traded goods (especially) in relation to domestic incomes. As a reduction in the level of real outlay less output ('net absorption') is necessary in order to achieve an improvement in the current account of the balance of payments, a general subsidy (or tax reduction) financed by borrowing will therefore to that extent not serve the same function as a devaluation. It is therefore likely to require complementing by a generally tighter monetary and budgetary policy than is a devaluation.

If one purpose, or the main purpose, of the devaluation was to act as a stimulus to domestic activity, this must be accounted among the worst possible ways to secure such a stimulus, as it is bound to raise the price level considerably. By contrast, a general subsidy or tax cut will stimulate activity in a way that will be among those least likely to raise the price level.

In short, there are alternatives to devaluation as a means of improving the current account of the balance of payments, and they are ones that are less likely to cause inflation and therefore more likely to continue to be effective in improving the competitive position of the country applying them. The more general measures—of reducing cost-push taxes or paying anti-cost push subsidies in all industries—would be preferable in terms of their generality (if their upward effects on the money supply were offset by either reductions in government spending or by increased bond sales). But more specific tax concessions or subsidies to those industries thought most likely to improve the balance of payments would have what some governments might see as the advantage of having a smaller effect in reducing tax receipts or in increasing government outlays; but the disadvantage would be that the government would have to select which industries to put in the category of beneficiaries—and one might doubt the ability of most governments to do this job of selection better than the market mechanism.

The Level of Tariffs as a Macroeconomic Instrument

If a tariff is increased or reduced, especially if the general level of a wide range of tariffs is changed, this may have important macroeconomic effects. It is just as important that this instrument should be correctly assigned to the objectives for which it is best suited as that other macroeconomic instruments should be used appropriately.

Externally we have come to think of a rise in a tariff as tending to improve the balance of payments on current account. This is because we have got into the habit of thinking of the exchange rate as fixed. This is no longer appropriate, if, indeed, it ever was. This does not necessarily mean that whenever a tariff is increased we have to assume that the currency appreciates at once (compared with the level that it would otherwise have achieved). But analytically this is normally the appropriate assumption to make, especially in a world where exchange rates are generally flexible, and where our effective exchange rate depends on all the various movements in exchange rates among different countries, which are affected by our tariff policy, among many other things. In any case, a decision to raise a tariff, or to impose other restrictions on imports, means that the exchange rate for our own currency can be, and must (in a world of reasonably flexible exchange rates) be assumed to be, stronger than would otherwise have been the case. For if we fail to appreciate after increasing the tariff, we are failing to apply the optimal macroeconomic policy; we are accumulating reserves unnecessarily.

IMPORT CONTROLS

Scepticism about the efficacy of devaluation as a means of improving the balance of payments has led a number of people to advocate the use of general import controls to effect a desired improvement in a country's balance of payments. These might have the advantage of operating in a speedier and more predictable manner than devaluation, so that if the alternative were a deflation of domestic demand which might need to be continued for a long time until devaluation had its desired effect on the balance of payments, it could be argued that the imposition of import controls might involve less loss of output and of economic welfare than would have to be incurred in the period during which domestic activity might have to be held down (pending the improvement in the balance of payments that would eventually be brought about by devaluation).

But import controls have very real costs, which are too well known to require extensive repetition here. They involve arbitrary decisions about which lucky importers should obtain the licences, and so obtain a windfall profit, enabling them to raise the price to the consumer without fear of competition from imported products (in contrast to a tariff or a devaluation, which at least leaves open some possibility of competition from imports if the domestic price is raised very high). They also usually involve arbitrary decisions about which products should be imported. Only if the licences were generally transferable amongst importers and as between commodities, and were sold in an efficient auction market, with the profits going to the government, would most or all of these objections be overcome.

Devaluation immediately raises the internal prices of those foodstuffs and materials whose prices are determined by world markets in which supply and demand forces operate quickly and smoothly. If these products are ones that quickly affect the cost of living to an important extent (as with foodstuffs imported into Britain) they are likely, especially given the existence of a close link between consumer prices and wage demands, to lead to a sharp rise in money incomes, which will quickly undo the effect of the devaluation to the extent that money wage rates rise correspondingly more rapidly.

If the goods excluded by the import controls were not ones whose prices would rise in proportion to a devaluation, and if they were not ones that figured to such an important extent in the consumer's budget, money wage rates might well rise less rapidly in response to the import controls than to a comparable devaluation. Furthermore, if raw and semiprocessed materials are admitted relatively freely under a regime of import controls, their internal prices may well rise less rapidly than in the alternative case of a devaluation. So far as manufacturers base their pricing policies on cost-plus factors, rather than on what the market will bear, even those protected by the restriction of imports may be less likely to put up their domestic prices as quickly as they would have done if the alternative of devaluation—with its immediate upward effect on domestic prices of imported materials—had been chosen instead.

The case for import controls may be reinforced if one believes that manufacturers exporting from a devaluing country are dilatory about raising their prices in terms of their own currencies after a devaluation. For if they are, and assuming that overseas demand for their exports is not very responsive to price changes (at least in the short or medium run) a devaluation may well have the effect (at least to begin with) of reducing the country's receipts in terms of foreign exchange.

But even if a country benefits by choosing import controls rather than devaluation in the short run, this advantage is likely to evaporate over time. In the first place, the import controls will themselves tend to raise costs within the country, and will, by increasing the effective extent of protection for the import-replacing goods competing with those excluded by the controls, tend to raise the price level within the country before long. Resources will be attracted towards those industries most protected by the import controls, and there is every likelihood that this will involve attracting resources away from industries in which the country could more efficiently have specialised if the stimulus to improving the balance of payments had been given to both sides of the accounts (by a devaluation), rather than simply by import controls. In any event, if the process of selecting the imports is left mainly to administrators (in an economy in which the consumer normally chooses the pattern of consumption in other respects) there is some presumption that the necessary improvement in the balance of payments will be made in ways that will inflict greater real costs on the consumer than if he had been allowed to choose where the economies in imports should be made. This is why a general system of auctioning of import licences (usable on any goods) or a uniform import-deposit scheme, would be preferable to a system of import controls as usually operated in the past.

Generally, however, import licensing as a balance of payments device is likely to involve at least as great a rise in the price level as a devaluation, for it is more likely to involve the waste of manpower and effort on the administration of the scheme, and more likely to result in a wasteful allocation of resources and a reduction of the incentive to produce efficiently what the public wants; so that it is therefore likely to reduce the available supplies of those goods and services in demand at a given level of activity. In these and other ways, therefore, the use of import licensing is likely to make it harder to keep down the price level and the rate of inflation at any given level of activity.

But if import licensing is widely believed to be superior to devaluation for a country in balance of payments difficulties, there is a real danger that countries may be tempted to resort to it, whatever its disadvantages as a means of overcoming an external deficit coupled with inflation. It is therefore imperative that attention should be focused instead on what can be done to improve the balance of payments by the adoption of a macro-economic policy mix that could have this effect without making inflation worse.

In general, import controls are even more likely than are high tariffs to reduce economic welfare and to raise the price level, at any given level of activity. Under conditions of stagflation, therefore, especially if output is being held down because of the government's fears about inflation, the reduction or elimination of import controls is likely to help to solve the problem; whereas any imposition or tightening of import controls is likely to place upward pressure on the price level and indirectly to make unemployment worse, as a result of governments being more reluctant to permit a high level of activity, because of this greater upward pressure on the price level resulting from the import controls.

Selective Import Controls and Selective Tariff Increases

Governments faced by high unemployment, especially those with a balance of payments that is not strong, have often had recourse to the use of selective import controls or higher tariffs to protect particular industries.

Obviously, if a tariff (or an import control) were justifiable for other reasons, the case for it would stand or fall on those grounds; but if a government decides to impose such limitations on particular imports as a means of maintaining employment in the particular industries affected, such a measure requires to be given special consideration here because it is likely to make stagflation worse.

Even if the only problem were a recession—that is, one without serious inflation at the same time—the provision of assistance to an industry in this manner would be indefensible. For if the general level of unemployment is too high, the aim should be to raise the level of demand and to absorb unemployed manpower in whatever industries can make the best use of it—and if total imports are higher than the country can afford, the price mechanism should be allowed to decide which imports shall be admitted; or, at worst, general import licensing (preferably through an auction) should be applied to determine the pattern of imports according to the government's assessment of the value of alternative products from a social viewpoint (or as the auction would determine). But if it is decided whether or not to admit particular products simply according to whether there is unemployment in a particular industry, this is likely to result in a reduction in living standards and not to reduce the level of unemployment.

Even if the tariff that was imposed was a flat-rate one on all imports, or on a wide range of imports, instead of a devaluation, this could be expected to distort the pattern of the country's production and consumption (further) away from that which would bring its consumers the highest level of economic welfare—at a given level of activity and a given state of its balance of payments. For the alternative of a devaluation would leave consumers and producers a greater degree of choice as to where the economies of consumption, and the changes in the pattern of trade and production, should be made to achieve the desired improvement in the balance of payments. If the aim in imposing the tariff was partly to reduce unemployment, the same argument applies. The country would be better off if it adopted some combination of measures that included devaluation, rather than a combination involving a higher general level of tariffs. As consumer satisfaction and economic welfare would be higher if tariffs were not increased, the likelihood of holding down the rate of inflation at any given level of activity would be greater, in the sense that a given level of money incomes would be accompanied by a higher real income if tariffs were not increased.

This argument is stronger if the government chooses to increase particular tariffs (rather than the general level of tariffs) in order to maintain employment in those industries where unemployment is greatest, or where employment is most threatened by competition from imports. This is partly because in this case a further effective limitation is imposed on the consumer's choice as to where the economies in consumption and imports shall be made; for the prices of the particular commodities being produced in these industries will then be forced up (relative to those of imports in general) as a result of the higher tariffs applied to these products. Moreover, at any given level of activity, this sort of tariff increase retains resources within the protected industry, whereas the absorption of some of those resources in other industries would have given greater consumer satisfaction, the industries that suffer most from competition with imports usually being among the least economic and most heavily protected. For any given level of activity, therefore, as a result of such a tariff rise employment will be higher in the assisted industry, but lower than it would otherwise have been in other industries. The resources of the country are thus being used less economically than they would have been in the absence of this particular tariff increase.

If the assistance had been given to the same industry by way of a subsidy instead of a tariff, this reduction in the efficiency with which the country's resources were being used would still have occurred; but in this case the other loss of economic welfare resulting from the imposition of a tariff—namely, that it discourages consumption of the protected product, by raising its price in the home market—would not occur.

Taken together, the effects of a tariff increase in reducing the economic welfare that the community derives from the pattern of its consumption, and also from the probable reduction in the efficiency with which it uses its productive resources, tend to reduce real income at any given level of activity, and to that extent make it harder to hold down the price level. Tariff increases—and still more so protection by import controls—thus tend to make inflation worse at any given level of activity.

But the position is far worse if the problem is stagflation, and if the government feels inhibited from taking expansionary action because it considers that the rate of inflation or the price level is too high. For in that situation, the imposition of a tariff or an import quota will reduce the satisfaction that consumers can derive from a given outlay of foreign exchange, and so raise the price level and worsen inflation over the period in question. This is likely to make the government correspondingly less willing to take expansionary action. Higher tariffs thus make stagflation worse on both counts; for they raise the price level and they therefore also make governments more cautious about adopting expansionary measures. Unfortunately, this effect of tariffs or import controls in increasing unemployment is usually concealed from the public by the frequent statements of the vested interests in question that the tariff or import restriction they are seeking will tend to 'reduce unemployment'—by which they mean unemployment in the particular industry for which they are concerned. As the indirect effect that such a limitation on a particular class of imports will have in increasing the general level of unemployment is much less obvious, the real nature of the macroeconomic effects of the tariff or import control usually remain unnoticed.

In any event, the additional unemployment and inflation that result from the imposition of a particular tariff or quota cannot, of course, in practice be traced to that particular restriction on an import. When inflation and unemployment rise, it will be some other industries that will consequently find themselves in greater difficulties, and which will often then also demand protection against imports, as the easiest way politically to obtain assistance (for the relevant exporters in other countries have no votes). Having given way to one import-competing lobby, a government will find it hard not to accede to the requests (or demands) of others. Each such concession will do something more to worsen stagflation; so that the process will tend to be cumulative. If applied in a number of countries simultaneously it will tend to reduce the level of world trade and also to make stagflation worse on a world scale.

By contrast, a government that moves in the direction of reducing or removing all those restrictions or tariffs on particular imports that cannot be justified in terms of their effects on the allocation of the country's resources will be able to reduce the price level at any given level of activity; and the measures it may consequently have to take to improve the balance of payments (at any given level of activity), if total imports consequently rise, will be ones that will tend to save imports in those directions where they can be most readily dispensed with—rather than where the imports are threatening those industries whose calls for help carry most weight. The consequent rise in real output available at any given level of activity will help to hold down prices, and so make the government readier to take the measures needed to promote recovery.

In marked contrast to the view often expressed that a recession is not the time for a reduction in protectionism, therefore, the fact is that in a stagflationary recession (at least) a reduction in the protection given to a particular (overprotected) industry can play a vital role in increasing economic welfare and so reducing inflation, thus paving the way to recovery, so long as the government has been inhibited from taking the appropriate stimulatory measures because it fears that it will thereby increase inflation. Any unwanted effects of the tariff reduction upon reserves or employment can and should be offset in the manner outlined earlier in this chapter by appropriate adjustments of budgetary and monetary instruments and the exchange rate.

7 International Aspects and Conclusions

The previous chapter considered the appropriate principles for the macroeconomic policy mix in a single open economy that was not large enough for it to be justifiable (in its own narrow interests) for it to take account of the effects of its actions on the rest of the world. But, in fact, the policies of each individual country have important effects on the economies of the rest of the world, even when those effects are not so large as to react back on the original government in a clearly discernible way. The success of the world economy in overcoming unemployment and inflation therefore depends on the decisions of all its individual governments. The world community thus has an interest in placing some degree of pressure upon individual countries to take into account the effects of their policies upon the rest of the world.

To some extent such pressures may be purely informal, through international discussions among officials and ministers, especially through the OECD. They may also spring from the observation of general rules of good conduct, agreed on through such bodies as the International Monetary Fund, or from more explicit undertakings, such as those given by a member government to the IMF when it makes substantial drawings from that body.

The present chapter considers the principles on which any such forms of international co-operation should be based, so far as their aim is to facilitate the maintenance of a high level of activity in the world economy with as little inflation as possible. The institutional machinery to give effect to such international co-operation will not be considered here; it may—and does—take many different forms, formal and informal, sometimes with and sometimes without some sort of effective sanctions to enforce the rules or agreements.

THE ROLE OF THE INTERNATIONAL MONETARY FUND

The formal role of the IMF in influencing members' policies has been exercised mainly (indeed, almost solely) through the conditions imposed by the Fund upon drawings made by members, especially when they have exercised a substantial part of their drawing rights, and so entered the later credit tranches of their drawing rights. For with such drawings the Fund normally insists on more rigorous commitments being made by the member concerned that it will pursue appropriate policies to correct its balance-of-payments deficit. Less formally, however, the Fund also exercises some influence on members' policies generally, by the regular review of each member's policies conducted by Fund missions, and through discussions at the annual meetings of governors, and of the Interim Committee, as well as through day-to-day contacts and discussions among the directors of the Fund, and between the staff of the Fund and officials and ministers of member countries.

The analysis of earlier chapters may be applied to considering the broad directions in which it would be most appropriate for the Fund to direct whatever influence it may have over members' economic policies.

Methods of Correcting External Deficits

The Fund should endeavour to see that a member which has a large balance-of-payments deficit corrects it in ways that will have as little adverse effect on its level of activity and on its rate of inflation as possible. Both of the orthodox remedies for an external deficit—deflation and devaluation—are subject to obvious deficiencies; for deflation operates by reducing the level of real demand—which is desirable only when demand is excessive, but not if the economy is operating at or below full employment (on any reasonable definition); whilst devaluation certainly tends to raise the rate of inflation in the devaluing country, whether or not it has much success in improving its balance of payments.

If there were no other ways to improve a country's balance of payments apart from deflation or devaluation (or the generally still worse alternatives of import controls and similar direct controls), this approach would be defensible. But the discussion of earlier chapters has stressed that the mix of macroeconomic measures applied by a country can affect its price level at any given level of activity, and so its international competitiveness. The aim should therefore be to see that a member country with an external deficit corrects its deficit by adopting a mix of measures that will hold down its price level and thus improve its current account, at any given level of activity, rather than by deflating to less than full employment, and preferably without the use of devaluation (which, even when effective in improving the current account, will make inflation worse in the devaluing country). If the world as a whole is maintaining full employment without serious inflation it may be sufficient to exert pressure on a deficit country (preferably with equal and opposite pressure being placed on surplus countries) to take action to correct its deficit. But in a world in which the problem is stagflation, any attempt by a deficit country to deflate will make world unemployment worse—at any rate if it starts from less than full employment.

Furthermore, any efforts to reduce its deficit may serve mainly to pass that deficit on to another country, and world trade and incomes are likely to be further deflated in the process, especially if this occurs by means of a reduction in the imports of the original deficit country. The attempt of many oil-importing countries to reduce their external deficits in the face of the oil price rises in the mid-1970s is an example of the way in which world trade and output may be held back by the attempts of countries to reduce their individual deficits, with adverse effects on the trade and output of the oil-importing countries, but little effect in reducing the current account deficit of this group of countries (as a whole) with the oil-exporting countries.

When there are simultaneously many countries with external deficits, attempts to correct these external deficits by deflation or by devaluations will not reduce world unemployment and inflation; indeed, such policies are likely to make both of these problems worse. Furthermore, restrictions on trade and high tariffs are likely to be among the corrective measures adopted by deficit countries; and these tend to depress world trade and to raise the price level at any given level of activity (by reducing the efficiency with which the world's resources are used), thereby making stagflation worse in both its aspects. It is clearly far preferable that those countries with external deficits should be assisted to eliminate them by measures that promote world trade and output; this means that the use of protectionist measures should be discouraged, and the operation of the economies of all member countries at near to full employment should be encouraged and facilitated.

The Policies of Surplus Countries

Obviously, the more liberal are the import policies of surplus countries, the easier will it be for deficit countries to eliminate their deficits. Liberal policies towards imports into surplus countries will also help to hold down the price level there, and so make it easier for such countries to take expansionary action (or to maintain full employment) without this leading to sharp increases in the price level. The combination of expansionary policies with import liberalisation is therefore appropriate for a surplus country operating at less than full employment; and the more such countries are willing and able to reflate, the better for the world as a whole.

Global Policies to Stop Stagflation

If the IMF adopts the viewpoint of the world as a whole, therefore, it should be placing pressure on deficit countries to correct their deficits in trade-creating ways, and by improving their competitiveness at any given level of activity, instead of by deflating, devaluing, or imposing restrictions or higher tariffs on their imports. It should also be doing what it can to encourage its other members to adopt expansionary measures coupled with the liberalisation of imports, so that the world can reflate out of its stagflation, with little or no upward effect on the price level or the rate of inflation. If the IMF remains so concerned about the risk of inflation that it fails to encourage its members to reflate, this will obviously tend to perpetuate stagflation. But unless the IMF simultaneously insists that its members—especially those in deficit—should choose a non-inflationary mix of measures as the means to achieve reflation, it runs the risk of the stimulus having more effect on prices than on output, and perhaps of petering out prematurely. The surplus countries are likely to be more willing to reflate if they are convinced that there are forms of stimulus available that operate by reducing costs (rather than by raising prices for finished products); and to that extent it is important that they, too, should be persuaded to adopt a mix of stimulatory measures that relies mainly on the reduction of cost-push taxes, coupled with a fairly tight monetary policy. But if they are willing to raise the level of activity even in the face of some upward pressure on their price level, it will be correspondingly easier for other countries to reflate without this leading them into balance-of-payments difficulties. It is also important that the measures of expansion chosen by deficit countries should be ones that will have little or no upward effect on their price level—as this will make it easier for them to reconcile reflation with the avoidance of balance-of-payments difficulties. The weaker is a country's balance of payments, and the more it is feeling inhibited from reflating by fears that reflation must cause more inflation, therefore, the more essential is it that it be persuaded to adopt a mix with lower cost-push taxation (or with cost-reducing subsidies) and a monetary policy that is tight enough to maintain sufficiently high interest rates to hold down the rate of inflation, and to assist it to avoid devaluations.

THE POLICY MIX IN DIFFERENT COUNTRIES

If individual countries attempt to apply the principles of macroeconomic mix suggested in Chapter 6, they may or may not do so in ways that will also help others to achieve success in these aims of macroeconomic policy. From the point of view of the world as a whole, the aim should be to see that those countries that are being least successful in achieving the main aims of macroeconomic policy, or in adopting the sort of mix of measures that is most likely to be successful, should change their policies in an appropriate direction. But that statement requires considerable elaboration before it can be used as a basis for international agreements—or as an indication that a country is acting as an internationally 'good neighbour'.

One principle is that those countries that are being least successful in reconciling a high level of activity with the absence of inflation should modify their macroeconomic mix, and the overall setting of their macroeconomic policies, in directions that would be more likely to achieve those aims. It is, of course, quite possible that a country that is being rather unsuccessful in achieving full employment without inflation may already be adopting a mix of measures closer to that prescribed than are other countries. But this might well be because its problems are greater than theirs (for one reason or another). There is, then, no presumption that every country should adopt exactly the same mix of measures; but there is a presumption that a country that is having less success in maintaining full employment without inflation ought to cut taxes, and also be prepared to have a tighter monetary policy.

If every country were satisfied with the level of its reserves, and were varying its policy measures (including its tariffs and exchange rates) in such a way as to keep its reserves more or less constant, the above prescription—that budgetary policy (especially tax policy) should be geared to the level of activity and monetary policy to the rate of inflation—would be appropriate and sufficient. But, in practice, at any given time there will be some 'deficit' countries which feel that their reserves are inadequate and their external accounts weak; and this view will often be shared by the rest of the world, which may well be placing pressure on them to improve their balance of payments. On the other hand, other ('surplus') countries are likely at the same time to have excessively high reserves or an excessively strong balance of payments; and, even if they do not themselves acknowledge this by taking appropriate steps to reduce their reserves (or their surpluses) the rest of the world is likely to be placing pressure, at least moral pressure, on them to do so.

In this case, there is a presumption that the countries with external deficits should adopt a mix with a tighter monetary policy than they would otherwise have chosen, and that the surplus countries should adopt a mix with a relatively easy monetary policy, until the deficits and surpluses are corrected.

But, as we saw in Chapter 6, this use of the monetary instrument to raise or reduce the reserves, or to influence the exchange rate, is really appropriate only for a limited period so far as it relies on affecting the capital account; for the effects that the consequent changes in capital flows will have on subsequent net international payments of interest and dividends will work in the opposite direction (in terms of their effects on the reserves) to that which will result from the original impact on capital flows. The proposed use of monetary policy mainly with an eye to affecting capital flows, and through them the level of the reserves, is therefore best suited to a pattern of surpluses and deficits that changes over the course of a period (such as the average trade cycle), or for handling problems that vary, over time and as between countries, on a fairly haphazard ('stochastic') pattern. The use of such a macroeconomic mix may well help to afford a country time in which to decide whether its problems are likely to be longlasting, and, if so, what other measures it should then take to correct them.

The sort of measures that one could recommend for a country with a more lasting surplus would be to reduce or remove any tariffs or other restrictions upon its imports or other payments to the rest of the world, preferably beginning with those that are the most restrictive. It should be prepared to offset simultaneously, by expansionary budgetary or monetary measures, any undesired downward effect that the reductions of tariffs (or the other forms of import liberalisation) may have on the level of activity. This combination of measures should help to reduce the rate of inflation in the surplus country, and also help to reduce or remove its surplus.

At the same time, deficit countries should be taking corrective action of an opposite sort; though the extent to which they will have to do so will naturally be less if the surplus countries are adopting measures of import liberalisation, or expansionary measures that raise their imports. Some of the corrective action by the deficit countries will, almost inevitably, take the form of adopting a less liberal trade policy than they would otherwise have followed, or the imposition of various controls on imports and limitations on other types of payments to other countries. Preferably, these restrictions should be of a general sort that makes use of the price mechanism, as they would then be least likely to raise the price level or to reduce the economic welfare of those countries applying them (and that of the world as a whole). Devaluation of their currencies may well constitute part of the necessary process of adjustment, though the risk that this may mainly increase their rate of inflation (unless other macroeconomic measures are strong enough to prevent this) should make one hesitate to recommend devaluation—whereas appreciation of the currencies of the surplus countries could reasonably be advocated both in the general interest and in that of those countries themselves.

The deficit countries might reasonably be expected to adopt a mix of measures incorporating lower tax rates, and so less cost-push inflation from that source, coupled so far as necessary with a lower level of government spending, and a high enough level of borrowing from the public, so that the overall level of demand would not be increased by the tax cuts.

So far as the deficit countries make use of a tighter monetary policy to improve their balance of payments, the net effect on capital flows will be the greater if the rest of the world is refraining from doing the same, and so far as surplus countries are taking the opposite action. But, for the world as a whole, if interest rates are not high enough to hold down the rate of inflation to the desired extent at full employment, there is a presumption that all countries, including the surplus ones, could usefully adopt a mix with a tighter monetary policy, especially if real post-tax interest rates are generally low or negative. In this case, the existence of reasonably high interest rates in the surplus countries would place pressure on the deficit countries to raise their interest rates still higher, in order to achieve a given improvement in the level of their reserves. So long as severe inflation persists in the world economy, therefore, the aim of encouraging countries generally to adopt a mix with tight money—and correspondingly lower tax rates—may suggest that even the surplus countries ought not to be too eager to use interest rate reductions with the aim of reducing their reserves (or of stimulating activity); and that the deficit countries, especially if they are among the most inflationary ones, ought to be even more reluctant to reduce their interest rates.

If the most inflationary countries are usually also the deficit countries—which is likely to be true on the average, though it is certainly not necessarily always true—the prescription that a country should tighten its monetary policy when inflation is severe and also that a country should do so when its reserves are too low (or its external deficits considerable) will lead these countries to adopt a relatively tight monetary policy (compared with that of other countries). Similarly, so far as the surplus countries are also the ones with least inflation, the obverse policy prescription would lead them to adopt relatively easy monetary policies, both on the grounds that this is appropriate as a means of reducing their surpluses and also on the grounds that as they have less inflation than the rest of the world it is not so necessary for them to tighten their monetary policy with the aim of reducing inflation.

WAYS OF REDUCING A SURPLUS

Is there any strong reason to prefer that a surplus country should reduce its reserves mainly by exporting more capital than that it should do so mainly by importing more from the rest of the world? The former solution will mean that the rest of the world still has available a larger proportion of its own current production to meet its own demands than it would if it were exporting more; and to that extent it should find it easier to hold down its price level at any given level of activity. But one of the problems of the deficit countries may be that they have an undesirably high level of unemployment, and are inhibited from raising the level of their activity (at least partly) because of their shortage of foreign exchange, and because of doubts about whether that can be remedied by devaluation, because of the risk that devaluation may result mainly in additional inflation. If so, the deficit countries may be more likely, and better able, to restore a high level of activity in their economies, without thereby causing themselves serious inflation, if the surplus countries raise the level of their imports, and thus increase the flow of foreign exchange to the deficit countries from this source; for the government of a deficit country may be somewhat readier to permit higher activity as a result of an increase in its reserves or in its foreign exchange receipts brought about in this way than as a result of an improvement in its external position that results merely from an improvement in its capital account. This is, moreover, a rational view for it to take, so far as it may expect the additional capital inflow to be only temporary; or to be likely to be quickly reversed; or to be more than offset before long by the additional flow of interest payments that will consequently have to be made to other countries.

In short, the helpful effect on the rest of the world will probably be greatest in the immediate future if the surplus country increases its capital exports; but a more lasting improvement is likely to occur if it raises the level of its imports, especially if the rest of the world is at less than full employment and is willing to permit higher levels of activity as a result of the increase in its exports to the surplus country. The nearer to full employment are the deficit countries, the less likely is it that their problems will be eased to a greater extent by an increase in their exports to the surplus countries (rather than by a rise in capital inflow from them); for a rise in the net exports of the deficit countries will then make it harder for them to avoid inflation. In that situation of close to full employment—provided that an increased flow of capital from the surplus countries made possible a higher level of imports than the deficit countries could otherwise have sustained—the deficit countries might prefer their deficit with the surplus countries to be reduced by means of a rise in the level of their capital inflow. In this case, therefore, international pressure placed on the surplus countries might reasonably be in the direction of encouraging them to ease their monetary policy (and to liberalise their capital outflow) rather than to increase their net imports. But, in practice, the surplus countries can usually help the rest of the world both by increasing their imports and by allowing or encouraging greater capital outflow; but the more lasting their surpluses are expected to be, the greater the emphasis that they should be enjoined to place on the former of these two means of adjustment.

Should Surplus Countries be Encouraged to Reduce their Exports?

When a country has a strong balance of payments, and if there are particular export products from that country that are causing problems for competing industries in deficit countries, political pressure is often placed on the exporting country to reduce its exports of these particular products. (This has also been done even where the exporting country in question has not had a surplus—especially with the aim of holding down textile exports from countries with relatively low living standards.)

Attempts to reduce a country's surplus by reducing particular exports from it are open to the same sort of objections as trying to reduce the deficit of a country by raising tariffs or imposing quantitative restrictions on particular imports: the products excluded are usually ones that would be especially likely to benefit the consumer in the importing country and help to hold down the price level there at any given level of activity; and the exclusion of these particular products means that correspondingly less effort will need to be made to correct a country's deficit by reducing its other imports or by increasing those exports from it in which its comparative advantage is presumably greater. In a situation of stagflation, where a government feels inhibited from restoring full employment by fears that this will generate a faster rate of inflation, it is essential that it make the most of the possibilities of international specialisation to import those goods that it can obtain at lowest cost by international trade, and then take measures to raise the level of activity in order to ensure that this does not lead to a higher level of general unemployment than would otherwise have occurred.

There is a more general objection to trying to correct a surplus by persuading the surplus country to restrict particular exports. It will generally be preferable for all countries concerned that any necessary corrections of surpluses and deficits should be effected by measures that maintain or increase the general level of trade, rather than by imposing new controls that limit the extent of the international division of labour. This means that the preference should be for encouraging the surplus country to liberalise its imports rather than for it to reduce its exports, and for the deficit countries to increase their exports, rather than to reduce their imports. It is especially important that surpluses and deficits should be corrected in such trade-creating ways when the world is concerned about high rates of inflation; for the better use of the world's resources that results from measures that liberalise (rather than restrict) trade will make it easier for all the countries concerned to hold down the price level and the rate of inflation at any given level of activity. It will therefore help to overcome the reluctance of governments to reflate, so far as they are inhibited from doing so by fears of a consequent increase in the price level. By the same token, measures that curtail the exports of surplus countries and the imports of deficit countries will tend to raise the price level, and so further encourage governments to dampen activity, in the hope of correcting the consequent rise in the price level.

Is There a Global Equivalent of a Monetary-Budgetary Mix?

International action can (at least in principle) increase the international liquidity of countries, by creating Special Drawing Rights in the IMF (SDRs). It is true that these are not 'money' from the point of view of individuals or of businesses (though it is possible at some future time that a decision might be made to make them available to private holders), but governments may regard them somewhat in the same way as individuals look upon their own holdings of money or other liquid assets. So far as this is true, governments may pursue more expansionary, or more inflationary, policies than they would choose if their holdings of international reserves (including SDRs) were lower.

In this sense, the creation of SDRs (provided that it does not lead for some reason to a fully offsetting fall in other types of international liquidity) may have effects on the level of world trade and world activity somewhat like those of a stimulus to activity within a country brought about by an addition to its money supply.

The question arises whether there is some internationally agreed equivalent to a measure of budgetary expansion within a country. One such measure might be a decision by a government to make available to another country international reserves that the donor would not otherwise have used. If total expenditure by the donor did not fall, or not by as much as the increase in total demand in the recipient country, this might act somewhat after the manner of a redistribution from rich to poor through the budget within a country. Again, a government, or the World Bank, might borrow on the world capital market and lend the proceeds to a country that is more likely to spend it than were the people who subscribed to the loan. The effects of this upon the world economy would be much like a rise in government spending financed by borrowing from the public. The borrowing in the world capital market would to some extent tend to raise world interest rates, and would to that extent tend to reduce the price level at any given level of activity. By contrast, newly issued SDRs might find their way directly or indirectly into the hands of a poorer country, which might then increase its spending, and which would then have correspondingly less need to borrow on world capital markets. If this meant that the country did in fact borrow less, world interest rates would be kept correspondingly lower.

Any contribution to an international organisation that leads to a net rise in the imports of the recipients is likely to raise the level of total demand in the world economy; and it will be sure to do so provided that the recipient organisation spends it and provided that the contributing country does not consequently reduce its own total expenditure, or its own net demand for imports from the outside world, to a fully offsetting extent. This will then be analogous to a redistribution through the budget within a country from people who were less likely to spend the sum in question (or likely to spend a smaller proportion of it in the period under consideration) than were the recipients.

There are, then, international analogues to budgetary as well as to monetary measures within a country. To that extent, an appropriately chosen international measure to raise the level of world activity without causing more inflation should be able to hold down the price level and the rate of inflation in much the same sort of way as can an appropriate choice of budgetary and monetary measures within a country. Borrowing in world capital markets by international organisations and governments for the purpose of lending the proceeds to countries where activity, and the demand for imports, is being held back by a shortage of international reserves is likely to be a less inflationary method of securing a given real stimulus than is the creation of additional international liquidity by such a means as the creation of SDRs.

TARGET-SETTING

Governments have often tried to adhere to 'targets' such as the rate of exchange, the level of interest rates, and the rate of growth of the money supply (which are not of inherent importance in themselves) because they believe that by doing so they will be more likely to achieve their fundamental economic objectives, such as full employment and a low rate of inflation. It would be far better if they were to concentrate upon working towards their fundamental objectives; for the achievement of one or more targets of this sort is not likely to ensure the attainment of the more fundamental aims of macroeconomic policy. The widespread popularity among governments of some sort of money supply targets in the mid-1970s can be best justified on the grounds that the fixation that so many governments displayed in earlier years upon the exchange rate and the level of interest rates had often caused them to permit excessive rates of growth of their money supply; so that the adoption of a fairly moderate target rate of growth for the money supply might in those circumstances constitute some sort of antidote or corrective to the former monetary excesses. It is certainly desirable that governments should watch the money supply (among other things), rather than that they should focus disproportionate attention on interest rates or the exchange rate. But now that they have passed through what may have been a necessary period when this antidote was being taken, it would be far better in future not to accept the aim of trying to fix any of these magnitudes at particular levels, but to try to adopt a combination of all the available macroeconomic instruments that will work towards the closest feasible approximation to full employment without inflation; and this requires a more sophisticated approach than trying to achieve target figures for particular magnitudes.

As we have seen in earlier chapters, the fundamental principle should be to vary each of the available instruments—taxation, government spending, and monetary policy—mainly with reference to that macroeconomic objective which the policy instrument in question is best fitted to influence. It is true that ideally it would be better to move all the instruments as quickly as possible to that combination of them which could achieve the best approximation to our basic objectives. But our present econometric knowledge is far from sufficient to enable us to do that. We have therefore generally to make successive variations in the available instruments in those directions that give the best hope of moving closer to their ideal settings. In practice, however, the actual policies adopted have often amounted to changing the setting of the various instruments in what are clearly the wrong directions; so that the principles suggested here should represent a clear improvement on what has often been done in the past, even though they would not be preferable to what might be feasible in a world with much greater econometric knowledge than we have at present.

Governments have often failed to reduce tax rates when their problem is clearly one of cost-push inflation coupled with unemployment; and have failed to keep the level of interest rates high enough in nominal terms even to provide lenders with positive real post-tax returns on financial assets, when the rate of inflation needed to be brought down. By contrast, the aim should be to bring down tax rates, but also to keep real interest rates high enough to restrain inflation, so long as stagflation continues. It has therefore to be asked whether these principles can be embodied in some sort of target-setting approach, so far as targets are thought desirable, or so far as a government may feel obliged to adopt targets, whether it wishes to have them or not.

One reason why some sort of targets may be adopted is that the International Monetary Fund has often insisted on targets being embodied in the commitments given to it by member governments which have been making use of a substantial part of their drawing rights in the Fund. Furthermore, some governments, notably that of West Germany, have taken the view that the announcement of a monetary target has some influence on wage settlements, as the parties to national negotiations consequently know in advance of their settlements that too high a rate of increase would lead to a higher level of unemployment, if the central bank adheres to the target that it has announced. It may also be argued that the announcement of an official money supply target (provided that there is public confidence that it will be achieved) may induce confidence on the part of the business world about this aspect (at least) of the government's intended policy. If this leads to a revival of business activity, a government may feel in some circumstances that it is worth accepting the consequent limitation on its freedom of action.

Whether we favour the use of targets or not, since many governments have seen fit to adopt and announce targets, especially for the money supply, we have to ask how any such approach can be made as consistent as possible with sound principles of macroeconomic policy-making. The rate of growth of the money supply (or the variant favoured by the IMF—the rate of Domestic Credit Expansion, or DCE, which concentrates on the internal influences upon the rate of increase of the money supply) may be consistent with any number of different combinations of inflation and unemployment, according to the particular mix of measures through which it is achieved. At one extreme, a rather slow rate of growth of the money supply might be achieved even with a very expansionary monetary policy, provided that this were offset by high rates of (probably cost-push) taxation. This would be likely to lead to a high rate of inflation, and consequently a low or negative rate of increase in the real money supply, which would inevitably bring also a relatively high level of unemployment. On the other hand, the same rate of growth of the nominal money supply accompanied by a low level of taxes and by substantial sales of attractive securities to the public could be expected to be consistent with a lower rate of inflation or with a higher level of activity, by virtue of the faster expansion of the real money supply resulting from the downward pressure of this sort of mix on the price level. The requirement is, therefore, to reinforce any monetary targets that may be adopted by adopting also some means of ensuring that real returns to the lender are kept up and tax rates are kept down, so long as inflation is too high, and especially if there is also substantial unemployment.

The other types of targets that have been most popular with the IMF do not seem well calculated to achieve these aims. One of them is the 'public sector borrowing requirement'—or what would in many countries be called the 'budget deficit'; that is, essentially the difference between the government's outlays and its current receipts (without taking account of its net borrowing). But a given rate of increase in either of these magnitudes would be consistent with many different levels of government borrowing from the public, and therefore with many different levels for the government's cash deficit, and so with various possible rates of growth of the money supply, so far as that depended on the net effect of government transactions. As we have seen in earlier chapters, a rise in interest rates, accompanied by a rise in government spending, may be expected to help hold down the price level at a given level of activity; and an upper limit to the public sector borrowing requirement would tend to reduce the scope for such a mix of measures to be adopted. It is the level of government borrowing from the banking system that needs to be restrained.

Furthermore, the difference between government outlays and current receipts can be struck at many different levels of government expenditure and taxation; whereas the aim should be to pitch the general level of the budget at a level that will contribute towards maintaining a high level of activity. It is true that if a target for the 'budget deficit' or 'public sector borrowing requirement' *and also* a target for the level of public spending, is accepted, that would imply a particular level for taxation (together with any other current receipts). If, however, more emphasis is given to the net figure for the budget than to that for government spending, the adoption of these targets may provide an incentive for the government to keep taxes at too high a level with a view to keeping down its net borrowing requirement. It would therefore seem to be far preferable to aim directly at bringing down the ratio of taxation to total output, whilst simultaneously adopting other targets that would keep government spending and borrowing from the public (respectively) at levels that would maintain both a high level of activity and a low rate of inflation. In such a complex of targets, a target rate of growth for the money supply may reasonably play its appropriate part (if targets are to be adopted at all). But to allow that particular target to dominate policy-making will serve no good purpose and, taken by itself, it is likely to lead to as many faulty policy decisions as did the earlier governmental fixations of the rate of interest and the exchange rate.

At the same time, the greater the number of targets a government adopts, the greater the risk of their proving to be incompatible with one another. For example, attempts to achieve a certain money supply target, whilst keeping key interest rates at a certain level, and trying to prevent the exchange rate from appreciating or depreciating beyond a certain level, must prove to be inconsistent except by mere chance. This risk will be correspondingly less, however, if the targets simply take the form of upper or lower limits (as the case may be): upper limits on tax as a proportion of total output: lower limits on post-tax interest rates (preferably *real* interest rates). If a target rate of growth for the money supply (or 'high-powered' money, or DCE) is adopted, it is therefore best that this should either be expressed as a range of maximum and minimum rates of growth, or preferably that it should be understood that the adoption of a single figure for the target rate of growth is to be interpreted reasonably flexibly, so as to imply a fairly narrow range about that figure.

Indeed, even if only one target (such as one for the growth of the money supply) is adopted, a reasonable flexibility in interpreting it is desirable, partly because of the difficulty a government has in achieving an exact figure for any such magnitude, and partly because it is difficult to foresee what rate of growth will be most likely to facilitate as close an approximation as possible to its macroeconomic objectives; and the desirable rate of growth of the money supply for achieving these aims does, as we have seen, depend on the setting adopted for each of the various policy instruments.

If the government is announcing a money supply target (in some form) partly with a view to affecting public expectations about its plans and so as to reflect its assessment of what the economy can reasonably expect, it is important that its willingness and ability to adhere reasonably firmly to the target should carry conviction with the public. Ideally, a government should hope to establish in the public mind the expectation that it will keep to its stated targets except when there are good reasons outside its control why it should depart from them: and it should in fact depart from them when it believes that there are valid reasons outside its control (consistent with achieving its macroeconomic objectives) for doing so, and which it can (and does) explain publicly. We may or may not be in sympathy with the use of targets; but it is important to try to see that any target-setting that takes place should be in those forms that have the greatest chance of doing good and which are least likely to do harm. If the target chosen is essentially one for the cash reserves of the banking system this is more likely to carry conviction, because a central bank has a greater chance of achieving this sort of target.

The 'Budget Deficit' as a Target

Excessive weight is often placed in public discussion, and even in government policy decisions, upon the difference between some measure of government outlays and current receipts. This is sometimes called 'the budget deficit', although to do so runs the risk of confusing this magnitude (which has little significance in itself) with the 'cash-deficit'—the difference between total outlays and total receipts including net government borrowing or lending.

In many minds the two magnitudes even seem to have become subconsciously equated, so that any reference to a rise in the 'budget deficit' (sometimes even more confusingly called simply 'the deficit') comes to be thought of as in some way an indication of the upward effect on the money supply resulting from government transactions. Yet a given 'budget deficit' (in the sense of government outlays less its current receipts) is obviously consistent with many different levels of the cash surplus or deficit, according to the level of net governmental borrowing from, or lending to, the non-bank public.

In any case, efforts to keep the government deficit—on these or any other definitions—down to a target figure are not likely to promote the achievement of the basic aims of macroeconomic policy. For a net difference between government payments and receipts can be struck at any number of different levels of the budget; so that it could be consistent also with many different levels of activity; that is, with many different levels of government spending or of taxation. A government that proclaims its intention to keep its deficit (on some definition) within a certain target or simply to 'balance its budget' is really telling us nothing that will help us to decide whether it is likely to have reasonable success in achieving any of the aims of macroeconomic policy. There is, moreover, no reason why a balanced budget (on any definition) should be the ideal setting for policy over a period of years.

There is another objection to placing emphasis on achieving any particular actual budget outcome (during any period of twelve months) that is even more decisive. For the level of activity itself affects the budget outcome, with a recession usually reducing tax receipts and increasing outlays on unemployment payments; naturally, if a government interprets the resulting movement towards a budget deficit as an indication that its policies are too expansionary, and consequently takes action to raise taxes or to reduce its spending, it will simply make the recession worse. Unless, therefore, the budget outcome that it uses (and the one referred to in public discussions) as a guide to policy is in a form that makes allowance for this effect on the budget of cyclical movements in the economy, it may well be tempted (or be persuaded by ill-informed public discussion of the actual deficit) to take budgetary actions that make matters worse. If it then again uses the consequently higher level of its actual deficit as a justification for taking further deflationary budgetary measures, there will be a further contraction of activity. Perhaps governments have been especially tempted to take such procyclical action during recent periods of stagflation, when their determination to stop inflation has led them to try to improve the state of the budget accounts, in the hope of thereby reducing inflation. But even if it is accepted that a movement towards reducing the budget deficit (at any given level of activity) can make a useful contribution towards reducing the rate of inflation, it must be some appropriate measure of the 'cyclically adjusted' or 'full employment', or 'constant employment', surplus or deficit to which the government directs its attention.

Indeed, some appropriately adjusted measure for each side of the budget (to abstract from the effects of the fluctuations of the economy upon the government's transactions) is really what is required as an indication of the setting of budgetary policy, rather than merely an adjustment to the net budgetary outcome (on any definition). For if it is accepted that high tax rates have some degree of cost-push effect (through any of the channels discussed in earlier chapters), the ratio of tax receipts to total output at full employment (or at any given level of employment) is a target magnitude of considerable importance. If, then, the government reduces its budget deficit by raising taxes to a very high level, it may have unwanted upward effects on cost-push inflation that may partly or wholly offset any contribution that may be made towards restraining the rate of inflation through moving the setting of its budget in the direction of a larger surplus (or smaller deficit).

So long as a country is suffering from high rates of inflation and high levels of unemployment, therefore, a government should have constantly in mind the need to reduce the level of tax receipts relative to total output. This is a more significant 'target' on which to focus than is any measure of the net state of the budget. But—as an indicator with a status subsidiary to that of tax rates (in relation to total output)—it may reasonably pay attention also to the net cash outcome of its budget, provided that this is calculated on a basis that allows for the 'feedback' effects on the budget accounts of the cyclical fluctuations in the economy. For the government's cash deficit (after due allowance is made for its borrowing from the non-bank public as well as its current transactions), is one important determinant of the money supply.

But even within the figure for the cash deficit a government will have to concern itself also with the analysis of its transactions between debt operations and government spending. Given the ratio of tax rates to total output, and the net cash deficit, a high level of both government spending and borrowing from the public may help to hold down the price level by keeping up nominal rates of interest and restraining the growth of the money supply. A government needs therefore to have in mind a subsidiary target of maintaining a high enough level of sales of securities to the non-bank public to restrain the growth of the money supply to an appropriate extent, and to keep the real return to the lender reasonably attractive (or at least positive in real terms after tax). But any such targets should be regarded as interrelated and equally important. For example, a larger excess of government outlays over tax revenue than would otherwise have been thought appropriate may be thoroughly acceptable if correspondingly greater efforts are made to sell more bonds to the public, by offering them on more attractive terms.

In short, a government that accepts a target such as one for the level of its expenditure or for its 'borrowing requirement', or an international organisation that imposes such targets, will not be adopting an appropriate set of indicators or aims for the achievement of a high level of activity with a minimum of inflation. Only a more complex set of interrelated 'targets' (if appropriately chosen), which would include the (maximum) ratio of taxes to total output, and the (minimum) real post-tax return to the lender, would be likely to promote this aim.

Targets Imposed from Outside

When a country is exercising a substantial part of its drawing rights with the International Monetary Fund, a condition of the use of these drawing rights is often that it should aim at particular targets, such as the rate of growth of its money supply—or in some cases of that part of it resulting from domestic influences (Domestic Credit Expansion or DCE), and that it should keep its 'budget deficit' (or 'public sector borrowing requirement') within certain limits. Subsidiary targets, such as restraint in total government spending are often also adopted.

One implication of the proposals made in this and earlier chapters is that these particular targets have various deficiencies. A particular rate of growth of the money supply, or of the DCE, may be compatible with many combinations of real growth rates and rates of inflation. A given public sector borrowing requirement may be consistent with a number of different levels of borrowing from the non-bank public, and also with different levels of taxation; whereas we have seen that the successful achievement of high levels of activity and low rates of inflation depends not only on the overall setting of demand (and so the degree of real stimulus given by monetary and budgetary policy taken together) but also on the particular mix of measures with which that stimulus is given. In the process of holding down the rate of inflation—as an aim in itself, and as likely to promote the improvement in the current account of the balance of payments (which is a main macroeconomic objective in a situation where a country is making a drawing upon the IMF)—it is important in the global interests for a country to keep tax rates low and real post-tax interest rates high, but with an overall setting of policy that maintains a high level of output, yet with as little inflation as possible. The IMF should therefore concern itself with achieving a degree of stimulus that will bring about full employment, and certainly not try to use a low level of demand as the means for improving a country's balance of payments. The interests of the world economy (which the IMF is presumably supposed to represent) require that each country be assisted to maintain a high level of activity without a high rate of inflation; and that it should not be inhibited from maintaining a high level of activity by concern for the state of its balance of payments.

But it is also of importance to the world economy that the mix of measures with which it does this should be one that holds down its rate of inflation, and does not make demands on the rest of the world by running external deficits on a scale that other countries are not prepared to finance. This implies the need to maintain pressure on a government to reduce or eliminate those tariffs and other restrictions on trade that distort its pattern of production in a way that reduces the level of its economic welfare, and that of the world generally. Pressure should also be placed on it to hold down the level of taxes and to make available to the public adequate supplies of attractive securities in order to remove the incentive for asset-holders in that country to try to bid up prices and money wage rates. A target for keeping up the rate of issue of attractive (preferably index-linked) government bonds, and for the payment of positive real rates of interest, could facilitate the working of the capital market and thereby help to hold down the price level at any given level of activity. It may also be true that when a country fails to maintain adequate positive real post-tax returns to the lender, this may stimulate the ratio of saving to income and thereby make it harder to maintain full employment.

Within an overall setting of policy that aims at full employment, then, the IMF should be exercising pressure on countries to hold down tax rates, and to hold up the level of securities sold to the public on terms that they find attractive (as well as to reduce tariffs and other restrictions on trade and payments). But a government will not necessarily be induced or encouraged to apply any of these principles (of a desirable macroeconomic mix to overcome an external deficit without stagflation) as a result of committing itself to a target for the rate of growth of the money supply (or DCE, or high-powered money), even if it also accepts a commitment about the level of its public sector borrowing requirement.

CONCLUSIONS

Finally, the main contentions and suggestions in this book should be stated, together with a number of propositions that have *not* been among the proposals made, but which some readers might otherwise mistakenly think to be part of the argument.

1. For the world as a whole, and as a broad principle also for individual countries, it has been argued that the combination of measures with which full employment (or, indeed, any level of activity) is achieved will have an important bearing upon the price level, and so upon the rate of inflation in the relevant period. It has *not* however, been argued that the level of activity has no bearing on the rate of inflation. In particular countries and situations a rise in the real level of demand may either raise or reduce the rate of inflation. But the precise mix of measures with which the rise in the level of demand is accomplished (or accompanied) will be at least as important (and, in the writer's view, much more important) in bringing about any consequent change there may be in the rate of inflation. It will always remain true, however, that if there is a rise in aggregate demand to a level in excess of what the economy will produce, this will be an inflationary influence. That effect may be offset by a change in the mix of macroeconomic measures in the appropriate direction; but so long as there is excess demand, any

given change in the macroeconomic mix will have less effect in holding down the rate of inflation than it would otherwise have achieved.

2. It has been argued that the adoption of a less inflationary mix (at any given level of activity) will facilitate the operation of any prices and incomes policy, or minimise the damage that such a policy is likely to do, by minimising the need to depend upon it to hold down the rate of inflation. It has *not*, however, been argued either that prices and incomes policies are useless, *or* essential, *or* harmless, *or* feasible, *or* unworkable. For different countries and situations, and for different types of incomes policies, any or all of these statements may be true (at one time or another). What *has* been suggested is that—whatever the contribution that may or may not be made by some forms of incomes policy—an appropriate, non-inflationary mix of the main macroeconomic instruments will be an essential element in any successful policy to reconcile high employment with the prevention of undue inflation.

3. The directions in which macroeconomic instruments should be changed with a view to affecting the main aims of macroeconomic policy should be such that each instrument is directed at influencing the objective for which it is most appropriate (or least inappropriate). If excess demand at full employment were the only reason why inflation could occur, this would not be of such importance; but when high unemployment and high rates of inflation occur together, the appropriate assignment of instruments to objectives becomes the touchstone of a well-designed macroeconomic policy.

4. The basic principle is that the setting of monetary policy should be directed towards achieving the desired effect on the price level—tightening it when inflation is too rapid. But that, simultaneously, budgetary measures should be used to maintain full employment, with cost-push taxes being cut (or anti-cost-push subsidies being paid) so long as the rate of inflation and the level of unemployment are simultaneously too high. It has *not* been argued that this (or any other) assignment of instruments to objectives is ideal; for if a government knows enough about the relative effects on each objective of all of its instruments it should be able to do better still. But it has been evident that many governments have been keeping tax rates high when cost-push inflation and unemployment were both excessive; and failing to offer to the public bonds carrying an adequate positive real post-tax return to the

lender; and that this is an example of a clearly inappropriate assignment of instruments to objectives.

5. In an open economy, it is unwise to try to use the exchange rate as an additional instrument. It is much more defensible to regard it as simply one of the channels through which an appropriate setting of the monetary and budgetary instruments will operate in bringing about the desired combination of employment and inflation. In an open, as well as in a closed, economy, therefore, a government should apply the principle of tightening monetary policy so long as inflation is too rapid, and using expansionary budgetary measures so long as unemployment is too low—preferably tax cuts, so long as cost-push inflation is considered to be excessive.

One implication of these proposals is that a high level of government spending does not necessarily lead to relatively high rates of inflation. It is true that if a reduction in government spending makes it easier to reduce cost-push taxes, restraint in government spending will to that extent be helpful. But there is the alternative of borrowing from the public, instead of imposing high taxes; so that if the arguments for a high level of government spending are considered sufficiently convincing, a high enough level of borrowing from the non-bank public may even make it consistent with a lower rate of inflation.

Finally, it has *not* been argued that the adoption of the sort of macroeconomic mix suggested is a 'panacea'—in the sense of promising success almost irrespective of the other elements of a government's policy. For if demand is permitted to be excessive even the best mix available will not solve the problem of inflation; and excessive wage increases (and increases in other money incomes) could undo the good effects of the best macroeconomic mix if people become too ready to allow rapid wage increases as a result of the knowledge that inflation could (in principle) be restrained by the adoption of the right mix of macroeconomic measures. Above all, if a government wastes its country's economic potential by misguided tariff policies, and other measures that affect the allocation of resources in an inefficient and uneconomic way, it is likely to increase the rate of cost-push inflation as a result of the dissatisfaction with the unnecessarily low living standards that people will consequently suffer.

In short, the adoption of the right sort of macroeconomic mix would enable governments to avoid many of the sort of mistakes they have made in recent years, which have intensified and perpetuated stagflation. It would not, however, enable them to escape the consequences of adopting misguided measures in other areas of economic policy. But in a period when high unemployment has been coupled with high rates of inflation to an unprecedented extent, whilst levels of taxation have been high, and the real post-tax return to the lender has been low or negative, an essential part of the remedy for this new macroeconomic problem is likely to be to reduce tax rates and simultaneously to sell sufficient amounts of attractive bonds to the non-bank public.

So long as governments try to fight inflation with unemployment the world will suffer unnecessarily. In the rich countries this may be largely a matter of a few more unemployed, often living on tolerable unemployment benefits, and some lapse below potential of average living standards that many feel to be already adequate. But for millions in the poorer countries the consequent check to world economic growth means real poverty and even starvation. For them it may well be a matter of life and death that governments everywhere should start at once to stop stagflation by cutting taxes, selling honest bonds, and removing barriers to trade.

> 'Do not despair—many are happy much of the time; more eat than starve, more are healthy than sick, more curable than dying; not so many dying as dead; and one of the thieves was saved. Hell's bells and all's well—half the world is at peace with itself, and so is the other half; vast areas are unpolluted; millions of children grow up without suffering deprivation, and millions, while deprived, grow up without suffering cruelties, and millions, while deprived and cruelly treated, none the less grow up.[1]

Appendix I: The Policy Mix and the Aggregate Supply Schedule

The two basic propositions on which the policy prescriptions in this book are based amount to saying that the aggregate supply schedule—the amount of production that will be offered at any given price level—will be affected by the particular mix of measures adopted.[1]

First, a high level of tax rates will mean that a higher price level will be required to call forth a given volume of output than would be required with lower tax rates. For if taxes are high a relatively small proportion of the price received for his production, or for his labour, finds its way to the producer or employee. Similarly if high tax rates reduce the productive efficiency of the economy, this, too, reduces the real amount of production available at a given price level, and thus requires a higher price level to call forth a given amount of production. High tax rates therefore shift the aggregate supply schedule upwards, which means that the price level will be higher for any given level of production than would have been true (all else being equal) at lower tax rates.

In the second place, a given real stimulus will shift the aggregate supply schedule upwards if it is provided by a monetary measure rather than by a budgetary measure—even a rise in government spending (and still more so if it were provided by a tax cut, for reasons discussed in the preceding paragraph). For a monetary stimulus operates by making people feel initially wealthier, in terms of their holdings of financial assets, especially money. If money were given to them as a transfer ('dropping it from helicopters') this is obvious; and if it is made available by the purchase of bonds from them, the bond-sellers must feel wealthier as a result—for otherwise they would not have been willing to sell the bonds to the government. In addition, all other bond-holders will also feel wealthier, as the market prices of their bond holdings will have risen as a result of the bond purchase by the government. As the initial result of the provision of a stimulus in this form, therefore, no one will feel less wealthy, and many people will consider their financial wealth to have been increased.

This consequent rise in their financial wealth makes producers and (actual or potential) employees less ready than they were before the monetary expansion to offer their output or services at any given price level. (If money dropped from helicopters is plentiful, people will not be so eager to work or to produce.) After a monetary stimulus is provided, therefore, the price level will have to be higher than before in order to call forth a given level of output; that is, the aggregate supply schedule will have shifted upwards.

By contrast, if the same real stimulus to activity had been given by a rise in government spending financed by borrowing from the public, there will either have been a fall in people's holdings of wealth (at the outset) or, at best, only a smaller rise than there was in the case of monetary stimulus providing the same real stimulus. For the budgetary stimulus we are considering operates by the government offering more employment and simultaneously borrowing from the public enough to finance it. It is true that the bonds sold to the public represent a rise in the wealth of the bond-holders (for otherwise they would not have bought them); but in this case there is no net rise in the money supply. However, the wealth of other bond-holders will have been reduced as a result of the fall in the current market prices of their bonds that will occur as a result of the bond sales, coupled with the rise in interest rates associated with the expansion in activity in the face of a fixed money supply.

In the case of the stimulus being provided by a rise in government spending (financed by borrowing from the non-bank public), then, there is no reason to expect the aggregate supply schedule to be raised by the provision of the stimulus; and, indeed, it may even be lowered. The price level will therefore not be raised from the supply side in the way that occurs when the same stimulus is provided by monetary policy.

Indeed, a rise in government spending financed by additional government borrowing from the public will actually reduce the value of financial wealth, on balance, if the demand for bonds is inelastic. For that means that the market price of bonds will fall more than in proportion to the increase in the number of bonds being sold to the public by the government. As the money supply is unchanged, on balance, by the combination of government spending and bond sales, this means that the nominal value of total financial wealth (money and bonds taken together) must fall in this case. This would result (on the basis of the argument given above) in a fall in the aggregate supply schedule as a result of an expansionary budgetary policy financed by a sale of bonds. The more difficult a government finds it to sell bonds—without thereby bringing about a substantial rise in the rate of interest—the more likely is it, therefore, that a mix of measures involving a rise in government spending and the sale of bonds to the public will reduce the price level at any given level of activity; and that a stimulus to activity provided by a mix of this sort will be consistent with little or no rise in the price level.

Appendix 2: The Functional Relationships Underlying the Policy Prescriptions

The functional relationships on which the argument of this book is based are as follows:

1. In a closed economy, the rate of inflation over a given period, $\pi = (\dot{P}/P)$, depends upon:

(a) *The level of activity* (Y) (relative to the capacity of the economy). Generally the rate of inflation is higher when the level of activity is higher; but at some low levels of activity, the decline in unit costs as industry recovers may reduce the rate of inflation during that period.

$$\frac{\delta\pi}{\delta Y} \gtrless 0$$

(b) *The expected rate of inflation* (x). This depends on various factors including the level of prices and rates of inflation experienced in the past, especially the recent past. A rise in the expected rate of inflation raises the actual rate of inflation.

$$\frac{\delta\pi}{\delta x} > 0$$

(c) *Tax rates* (t). Most or all taxes have some degree of cost-push effect. It is true that high taxes also depress activity, and this will generally tend to hold down the rate of inflation; but that consideration has been covered under (a) above.

$$\frac{\delta\pi}{\delta t} > 0$$

(d) *The money supply* (M). At any given level of activity and tax rates, a mix that includes a relatively high, or rapidly rising, money supply will tend to raise the rate of inflation. This may well operate partly, or even wholly, by raising the expected rate of inflation. But it may also directly raise the price level, as it raises the aggregate supply schedule: for the higher level of financial wealth (in nominal terms) that results from the more expansionary setting of monetary policy means that producers will require higher prices to persuade them to produce a given output, and wage-earners will require (and be likely to obtain) higher money wage rates to supply a given amount of labour, by comparison with a mix involving a more restrictive budget and a less expansionary monetary policy.

$$\frac{\delta\pi}{\delta M} > 0$$

(e) *Rates of Interest* (r). To a large extent this is covered under (d). For a relatively rapid rise in the money supply will tend to hold down nominal rates of interest. This will increase the attractiveness of goods compared with financial assets (at any given level of activity), and this will tend to raise their price level. But nominal rates of interest do not always quickly or fully adjust to a more rapid rise in the money supply or the expectation of a higher rate of inflation; and they may rise or fall with changing views in the bond market. These considerations are therefore not necessarily fully covered under (b) and (d) above.

$$\frac{\delta\pi}{\delta r} < 0$$

Putting together all these considerations, the rate of inflation depends on the level of activity, the expected rate of inflation, the level of tax rates, the level of the money supply and (negatively) on the rate of interest.

$$\pi\,(=P/P) = f(\underset{\pm}{Y}, \underset{+}{x}, \underset{+}{t}, \underset{+}{M}, \underset{-}{r}) \qquad (1)$$

2. The policy implications are that an economy that wishes to raise the level of activity or employment by a certain amount, but which wishes to minimise the upward pressure on the price level when it does so, should give the stimulus with as low a level of tax rates as possible and as low a level of the money supply as possible.

If one signifies the relative upward effect on activity by δY and the upward effect on inflation by $\delta\pi$, the relative advantage of stimulating activity by one instrument rather than another will be as follows.

Cuts in tax rates are denoted by $-\delta T$; a rise in government spending on goods and services by δG; and a purchase of bonds from the public (or any other form of easier monetary policy) by $-\delta B$ (that is, a fall in the amount of bonds in the hands of the public).

$$\frac{-\dfrac{\delta Y}{\delta T}}{-\dfrac{\delta \pi}{\delta T}} > \frac{\dfrac{\delta Y}{\delta G}}{\dfrac{\delta \pi}{\delta G}} > \frac{-\dfrac{\delta Y}{\delta B}}{-\dfrac{\delta \pi}{\delta B}} \qquad (2)$$

This indicates that, of the three, a monetary stimulus will have the greatest upward effect on the price level, and a tax cut the least upward effect, for any given real stimulus to the level of activity (a rise in government spending being intermediate between the other two). In other words, if the aim is to reduce the rate of inflation, this can be done with the least downward effect on activity if the instrument used is a sale of bonds to the public (or any other form of a tighter monetary policy); whereas the use of a high level of taxes for this purpose will have the greatest downward effect on activity for such effect as it may have in holding down the price level (a reduction in government spending being intermediate in this respect).

$$\frac{-\dfrac{\delta \pi}{\delta B}}{-\dfrac{\delta Y}{\delta B}} > \frac{\dfrac{\delta \pi}{\delta G}}{\dfrac{\delta Y}{\delta G}} > \frac{-\dfrac{\delta \pi}{\delta T}}{-\dfrac{\delta Y}{\delta T}} \qquad (2a)$$

3. In an open economy also, the relative effects outlined above are relevant. But, in addition, the level of the reserves, or the exchange rate, will be affected in varying degrees by each of the instruments (for a given change in activity). If we use δR to mean either a rise in the level of the reserves or an appreciation, R rises when the price level or the rate of inflation falls, because of the consequent improvement in the current account.

$$\frac{\delta R}{\delta \pi} > 0$$

In addition, the reserves rise as a result of an increase in interest rates, so far as this stimulates capital inflow.

$$\frac{\delta R}{\delta r} > 0$$

The unfavourable movement in the reserves (or the depreciation) resulting from an easing of monetary policy is greater than that which results from a reduction in taxation having the same upward effect on activity. This is for two reasons: the easier monetary policy is more inflationary (see equation 2), so that it has a greater adverse effect on the current account, and it also discourages capital inflow.

If, therefore, we choose alternative variations of government spending (δG) tax cuts ($-\delta T$) and bond purchases ($-\delta B$) in such a way as to have the same upward effect on activity, but we wish to use the form of stimulus that will have the least unfavourable effect on the reserves, tax cuts will be preferable to the others; for they will have least adverse effect on the reserves, because they reduce cost-push inflation; whereas a monetary expansion will have the greatest adverse effect on the reserves, as it worsens the current account through raising the rate of inflation and also reduces capital inflow.

$$\frac{-\dfrac{\delta Y}{\delta T}}{-\dfrac{\delta R}{\delta T}} > \frac{\dfrac{\delta Y}{\delta G}}{\dfrac{\delta R}{\delta G}} > \frac{-\dfrac{\delta Y}{\delta B}}{-\dfrac{\delta R}{\delta B}} \qquad (3)$$

Conversely, if the aim is to improve the reserves with the least downward effect on activity, monetary policy—that is, bond sales (δB)—will achieve a given rise in the reserves with the least downward effect on activity.

$$\frac{\frac{\delta R}{\delta B}}{\frac{\delta Y}{\delta B}} > \frac{-\frac{\delta R}{\delta G}}{-\frac{\delta Y}{\delta G}} > \frac{\frac{\delta R}{\delta T}}{\frac{\delta Y}{\delta T}} \tag{3a}$$

The relative effects on the price level of the two instruments G and T are the same as their relative impact on the reserves (since this depends entirely on their respective effects on the rate of inflation). There is therefore nothing to choose between them in respect of their relative impact on those two objectives.

Thus:

$$\frac{\frac{\delta R/-\delta G}{\delta Y/-\delta G}}{\frac{\delta \pi/-\delta G}{\delta Y/-\delta G}} = \frac{\frac{\delta R/\delta T}{\delta Y/\delta T}}{\frac{\delta \pi/\delta T}{\delta Y/\delta T}} \tag{4}$$

Monetary measures will have a bigger downward effect on prices (for a given reduction in activity) than will either of the budgetary measures. But in addition to this advantage of monetary policy for affecting the balance of payments through the price level, it also has the advantage of effecting an improvement through the capital account, so that its superiority over the budgetary instruments for this purpose is still greater.[1]

$$\frac{\frac{\delta R/\delta B}{\delta Y/\delta B}}{\frac{\delta \pi/\delta B}{\delta Y/\delta B}} > \frac{\frac{\delta R/\delta T}{\delta Y/\delta T}}{\frac{\delta \pi/\delta T}{\delta Y/\delta T}} = \frac{\frac{\delta R/-\delta G}{\delta Y/-\delta G}}{\frac{\delta \pi/-\delta G}{\delta Y/-\delta G}} \tag{5}$$

or, more simply,

$$\frac{\delta R/\delta B}{\delta \pi/\delta B} > \frac{\delta R/\delta T}{\delta \pi/\delta T} = \frac{\delta R/-\delta G}{\delta \pi/-\delta G} \tag{5a}$$

Notes and references

Chapter 2

1. See A. W. Phillips, 'The relationship between unemployment and the rate of change of money wage rates in the United Kingdom', *Economica* (November 1958).

Chapter 3

1. Colin Clark pointed out many years ago that there was an association between high rates of inflation and high ratios of taxes to national income—'Public Finance and the Value of Money', *Economic Journal* (1945).
2. See John Pitchford and Stephen J. Turnovsky, 'Income Distribution and Taxes in an Inflationary Context', *Economica* (August 1975), and 'Some Effects of Taxes on Inflation', *Quarterly Journal of Economics* (November 1976); also R. E. Rowthorn, 'A Conflict Theory of Inflation', *Cambridge Journal of Economics,* 2 (1977).
3. In other words, the mix with a larger money supply shifts the aggregate supply schedule upwards (see Appendix 1).
4. I am indebted to Ian McDonald for pointing out to me the effect of the 'easy money' type of mix upon the natural rate of unemployment.
5. These issues have been discussed by Walter Eltis and R. Bacon in *Britain's Economic Problem: Too Few Producers* (Macmillan, 1976).

Chapter 4

1. R. Solow and Alan S. Blinder, 'Does Fiscal Policy Still Matter'? *Journal of Monetary Economics* (November 1976).
2. See George Yarrow, 'Growth Maximisation and the Firm's Investment Function', *Southern Economic Journal* (April 1975).
3. Warren E. Weber in 'The Effects of Interest Rates on Aggregate Consumption', *American Economic Review* (September 1970), found evidence of consumption reacting in this way to interest rate changes in the USA.
4. *Bibliographical note.* The present writer has found two published references where the authors advocate the simultaneous use of expansionary budgetary policy and contractionary monetary policy to overcome stagflation. The first is by Robert A. Mundell in F. Machlup (ed.), *Economic Integration, Worldwide, Regional, Sectoral* (Proceedings of the International Economic Association Congress in Budapest, 1974) (Macmillan, 1976), page 203. I quote the passage in full:

> The appropriate policy mix for inflationary recessions requires a split of our monetary and fiscal instruments, using expansionary fiscal policy to cope with excessive unemployment, and monetary restraint to curb excessive inflation.

> Tight money and fiscal ease lower both inflation and unemployment, and tend to improve the capital account of the balance of payments more than they hurt the balance of trade. The two financial instruments have differential effects on inflation and unemployment. The differences arise because of the homogeneous character of wage, price and money changes, differences between national and international impacts, aggregate supply *versus* aggregate demand changes and even expectational effects. And just as monetary and fiscal policies are totally different instruments, so the rate of inflation and the level of unemployment are differential targets. Tax policy has a comparative advantage in altering the equilibrium level of unemployment and the rate of monetary expansion on the rate of inflation.

Although Mundell does not spell out the nature of the differential effects to which he refers, some of them at least appear to be those on which the arguments of the proposals in the present book are based.

Thomas F. Dernburg has also advocated something similar, in 'Inflationary Recession and the Appropriate Mix of Policy', *IMF Staff Papers* (1974); and in Thomas F. Dernburg and Duncan M. McDougall, *Macroeconomics* (McGraw-Hill, 5th edition, 1976), pages 328–43. His prescription for dealing with stagflation is the same, but he derives it from considering only a situation where the stagflation is due to the upward effects of a personal income tax upon wage settlements. He makes no mention of the possibility of indirect taxes having a similar upward effect on money wage rates; nor of the possibility of the price level being raised by the cost-push effects on the prices of finished goods of taxes upon business inputs (including taxes on employment); though his diagram could presumably be adapted to illustrate these effects also. Nor does he refer to the possible upward effects on the price level that may result from the uneconomic use of resources and from the adverse effects on incentive that may result from high rates of taxation. (Furthermore, he does not consider the possibility that low or negative real interest rates and a relatively high money supply may have upward effects on the price level at any given level of activity.)

Chapter 6

1. I am indebted to David Vines for saving me from several errors in this chapter.
2. It is important always to consider the effects of exchange rate changes in terms of foreign exchange (and also in terms of their real effects on domestic activity or employment). For if the unit employed is the currency of the devaluing country itself, this is in effect using a measuring rod that is itself changing in size as a result of the devaluation. In other words, if there were no real change as a result of the devaluation, a calculation in terms of the devaluing currency would show rises in both imports and exports, and a rise in the deficit (if there were a deficit initially). It is essential to separate this 'measuring rod' effect from the matters of real interest—which are the effects on the country's reserves and on its level of employment. Discussion and calculations of the effects of exchange rate changes should therefore be in terms of some major currency whose parity against the average of other currencies has not changed appreciably, or, preferably, in terms of some weighted average of currencies (such as the SDR (Special Drawing Rights) unit of the International Monetary Fund). Alternatively, the calculation might be in terms of the predevaluation (or preappreciation) value of the currency

whose parity had altered; thus a ten per cent rise in the reserves, or deficit (as normally measured in its own currency) would represent no real change after a ten per cent devaluation.

3. See *Marina v. N. Whitman*, 'Global Monetarism and the Monetary Approach to the Balance of Payments', *Brookings Papers in Economic Activity* (December 1975).

4. It is also likely to give excessive protection to those industries that are most obviously competitive with imports, such as manufacturers, and relatively inadequate assistance to industries such as live entertainment, which on the face of it appear to be 'non-traded' items.

5. For an algebraic formulation of these principles, see Appendix 2.

6. For a survey of recent literature on this subject see Dale W. Henderson, 'Modeling the Interdependence of National Money and Capital Markets', *American Economic Review; Papers and Proceedings* (February 1977).

7. See Rudiger Dornbusch and Paul Krugman, 'Flexible Exchange Rates in the Short Run', *Brookings Papers in Economic Activity*, 3 (1976).

Chapter 7

1. From the final speech of Tom Stoppard's *Jumpers* (Faber, 1972), page 87.

Appendix 1

1. I am indebted to Ian McDonald and David Vines for pointing this out to me.

Appendix 2

1. I am indebted to David Vines for considerable assistance with the preparation of this Appendix.

Index